M000044290

COOKSHELF
Indian

Shehzad Husain

This is a Parragon Book
This edition published in 2000
Parragon
Queen Street House
4 Queen Street
Bath BA1 1HE,UK

Hardback ISBN: 0-75254-135-8
Paperback ISBN:0-75254-141-2

Printed in China

Note
Cup measurements in this book are for American cups. Tablespoons are
assumed to be 15 ml. Unless otherwise stated, milk is assumed to be full fat,
eggs are medium and pepper is freshly ground black pepper.

Contents

Introduction

The subcontinent of India and Pakistan is an area of some 4 million square kilometres and comprises very many different cultures and religions, of which the main groups are the Hindus and Muslims, within each of which are smaller sects, the Parsees and the Christians. All of these have influenced the eating habits and tastes of the various ethnic communities throughout the subcontinent. The food eaten in the north, for example, differs considerably from that of the south. The people of the north, which is a wheat-growing area, prefer Indian breads such as *chapatis* or *paratas* as their staple, while rice which is grown in many of the southern states is preferred by the southerners.

Muslims are the meat-eating population of India, but for religious reasons they do not eat anything derived from the pig, which is considered unclean. Hindus, a vast majority of whom are vegetarians, are forbidden to eat beef, because the cow is considered to be a sacred animal.

Spices and herbs have been used to flavour food for thousands of years in the East, and India has for centuries been an important source of spices for Western nations. Yet it is only in the last twenty years or so that the majority of people in the West have become generally aware of our spicy cuisine. This may well be due in part to the great ease of communication, by jet travel, with India, and the fact that many people are now travelling to the Indian subcontinent where they have the opportunity to taste a variety of dishes on their home ground. But most of all it has been due to the proliferation of Indian restaurants in towns and cities throughout the world and, in particular, the British Isles. The Indian communities which have settled in Britain and in other countries have not only preserved their own culture and eating habits but, by setting up their own trading systems for specialist ingredients, made real Indian cookery possible on a far wider scale than would have been possible even ten years ago.

Indian dishes are wonderfully good-tempered, in that very few of them need any last minute attention whatsoever (maybe just sprinkling with a garnish in some cases); the majority of the dishes can be made well in advance and will freeze successfully – and indeed, some actually improve through keeping; others will usually keep in a refrigerator for a day or so until you are ready to reheat them. Also, because it is perfectly correct to serve all the dishes, other than dessert, at once, the cook need not leap up from the first course in order to get the main course organised – everything can go on the table at the beginning of the meal.

What about the question of spiciness? Must you spend a fortune on a cupboard full of exotic items before you even begin? And how do you gauge what degree of 'hotness' will be acceptable to your guests? Almost all the recipes in this book contain spices of one sort or another, but not necessarily a wide selection for each individual dish. However, if you know you like Indian food and are likely to be cooking it on a regular basis, it is advisable to buy a basic range of spices for your own convenience (see Store-cupboard Items, opposite) which will see you through a good variety of recipes. Then build up gradually as you start to try others. Hotness often depends on the amount of chilli, in whatever form: fresh chillies, which I use a great deal for garnish as well as in curry sauces, dried chillies and ground chilli (chilli powder also known as cayenne pepper). It is well to under- rather than over-estimate the amount of chilli you will need until you gain some experience in Indian cooking, and to remember that you can take some of the sting out of chilli pods by scraping out the seeds. But, most importantly, do not make the mistake of thinking that all Indian curries must be red-hot to be 'authentic'. We usually serve a variety of mild and hot dishes at any given meal. You should always plan your meals to include both milder and hotter dishes, because there is no point in destroying your guests' palates for your more delicately-flavoured dishes by killing their taste buds with chilli.

EQUIPMENT FOR INDIAN COOKING

Your own kitchen will probably be equipped already with everything needed for cooking a full range of Indian dishes. Some good-quality saucepans, with thick bases, and a heavy-bottomed frying-pan (skillet) are essential, and you will want some wooden spatulas and, ideally, a perforated spoon for stirring rice, to use with them. You will want at least one good, sharp knife and for measuring some spoons and a jug.

For grinding spices you can use a pestle and mortar, a coffee grinder or food processor, or a rolling-pin: in many Indian households a flat, heavy grindstone and something like a rolling-pin (called a *mussal*) are still considered the best solution.

STORE-CUPBOARD ITEMS

Your basic stock of spices should include fresh ginger and garlic, chilli powder, turmeric, cardamom, black pepper, ground coriander and cumin. The powdered spices will keep very well in airtight containers, while the fresh ginger and garlic will keep for 7-10 days in the refrigerator. Other useful items, to be acquired as your repertoire increases, are cumin seeds (black as well as white), onion seeds, mustard seeds, cloves, cinnamon, dried red chillies, fenugreek, vegetable ghee and garam masala (a mixture of spices that can either be bought ready-made or home-made in quantity for use whenever required).

USING SPICES

You can use spices whole, ground, roasted, fried, or mixed with yogurt to marinate meat and poultry. One spice can alter the flavour of a dish and a combination of several can produce different colours and textures. The quantities of spices shown in the recipes are merely a guide. Increase or decrease them as you wish, especially in the cases of salt and chilli powder, which are a matter of taste.

Many of the recipes in this book call for ground spices, which are generally available in supermarkets as well as in Indian and Pakistani grocers. In India we almost always grind whole spices ourselves, and there is no doubt that freshly ground spices do make a noticeable difference to the taste.

Some recipes require roasted spices. In India, this is done on a *thawa*, but you can use a heavy, ideally cast iron frying-pan (skillet). No water or oil is needed: the spices are simply dry-roasted whole while the pan is shaken to stop them burning on the bottom of the pan.

Remember that long cooking over a lowish heat will improve the taste of the food as it allows the spices to be absorbed. This is why re-heating dishes the following day is no problem for most Indian food.

Meat & Fish

There is a wide variety of meat recipes in this chapter, and in most cases the meat is lamb. I prefer to use leg of lamb, as it is much less fatter than shoulder, but if you like shoulder I suggest you combine it with an equal proportion of leg, which works very well. In some of the recipes beef (braising steak, for example) may be substituted for lamb, but if you do this you will need to allow a little extra cooking time.

In India, chicken is expensive and is therefore considered a special-occasion meat. Indians always cook chicken skinned and cut into small pieces. If the chicken weighs about 1.5 kg/3 lb 5 oz it should be cut into about 8 pieces, unless you are making Tandoori Chicken, when chicken quarters look a lot better and are more appropriate. Ask your local butcher to skin, cut and bone the chicken for you.

India may not be thought of as a great fish-eating nation, but there are certain parts of it, notably Bengal and around the city of Karachi, where fish is very popular. Indeed, the staple diet of the Bengalis is fish and rice.

Hot Spicy Lamb in Sauce

Serves 6–8

INGREDIENTS

175 ml/6 fl oz/³/4 cup oil
1 kg/2 lb 4 oz lean leg of lamb,
　　cut into large pieces
1 tbsp ground garam masala
5 medium onions, chopped
150 ml/5 fl oz/²/3 cup yogurt
2 tbsp tomato purée (paste)
2 tsp fresh ginger root, finely
　　chopped
2 tsp fresh garlic, crushed

1¹/2 tsp salt
2 tsp chilli powder
1 tbsp ground coriander
2 tsp ground nutmeg
900 ml/1¹/2 pints/3³/4 cups
　　water
1 tbsp ground fennel seeds
1 tbsp paprika
1 tbsp *bhoonay chanay* or
　　gram flour

3 bay leaves
1 tbsp plain (all-purpose) flour
naan breads or paratas, to
　　serve

TO GARNISH:
2-3 green chillies, chopped
fresh coriander (cilantro)
　　leaves, chopped

1 Heat the oil in a pan and add the meat and half of the garam masala. Stir-fry the mixture for 7-10 minutes until the meat is well coated. Using a perforated spoon, remove the meat and set aside.

2 Fry the onions in the pan until golden. Then return the meat to the pan, reduce the heat and simmer, stirring regularly.

3 In a separate bowl, mix the yogurt and tomato purée (paste), ginger, garlic, salt, chilli powder, ground coriander, nutmeg and the rest of the garam masala. Pour this mixture over the meat and stir-fry, mixing the spices well into the meat, for 5-7 minutes.

4 Add half of the water, then the fennel, paprika and *bhoonay chanay* or gram flour. Add the remaining water and bay leaves, lower heat, cover and cook for 1 hour.

5 Mix the flour in 2 tbsp of warm water and pour over the curry. Garnish with the chillies and the coriander (cilantro); cook until the meat is tender and the sauce thickens. Serve with Naan (see page 178) or Paratas (see page 174).

Tomatoes Cooked with Meat & Yogurt

Serves 2-4

INGREDIENTS

1 tsp garam masala
1 tsp fresh ginger root, finely
   chopped
1 tsp fresh garlic, crushed
2 black cardamoms
1 tsp chilli powder
1/2 tsp black cumin seeds
2 x 2.5 cm/1-inch cinnamon
   sticks

1 tsp salt
150 ml/5 fl oz/2/3 cup natural
   yogurt
1/2 kg/1 lb 2 oz lean cubed
   lamb
150 ml/1/4 pint/2/3 cup oil
2 onions, sliced
600 ml/1 pint/2 1/2 cups water

2 firm tomatoes, cut into
   quarters
2 tbsp lemon juice

TO GARNISH:
fresh coriander (cilantro)
   leaves, chopped
2 green chillies, chopped

1 In a large bowl, mix together the garam masala, ginger, garlic, cardamoms, chilli powder, black cumin seeds, cinnamon sticks, salt and yogurt until well combined.

2 Add the meat to the bowl and mix well to coat the meat. Set aside.

3 Heat the oil in a large saucepan and fry the onions until golden brown.

4 Add the meat to the pan and stir-fry for about 5 minutes. Reduce the heat, add the water, cover and simmer for about 1 hour, stirring occasionally.

5 Add the tomatoes and sprinkle with lemon juice. Leave to simmer for a further 7-10 minutes.

6 Garnish with coriander (cilantro) leaves and green chillies. Serve hot.

COOK'S TIP

Khormas *are slowly braised dishes, many of which are the rich and spicy, Persian-inspired Mogul dishes served on special occasions. In a properly cooked* khorma*, prime, tender cuts of meat are used, and the small amout of cooking liquid is absorbed back into the meat to produce a succulent result.*

Lamb with Onions & Dried Mango Powder

Serves 4

INGREDIENTS

4 medium onions	1 tsp chilli powder	600 ml/1 pint/2^1/$_2$ cups water
300 ml/^{1}/$_2$ pint/1^1/$_4$ cups oil	1 pinch turmeric	1^1/$_2$ tsp *aamchoor* (dried
1 tsp fresh ginger root, finely	1 tsp salt	mango powder)
chopped	3 green chillies, sliced finely	fresh coriander (cilantro)
1 tsp fresh garlic, crushed	450 g/1 lb leg of lamb, cubed	leaves

1 Using a sharp knife, chop 3 onions finely.

2 Heat 150 ml/^{1}/$_4$ pint/^{2}/$_3$ cup of the oil in a pan and fry the onions until golden brown. Reduce the heat and add the ginger, garlic, chilli powder, turmeric and salt to the pan. Stir-fry the mixture for about 5 minutes, then add 2 of the chillies.

3 Add the meat to the pan and stir-fry the mixture for a further 7 minutes.

4 Add the water to the pan, cover and cook over a low heat for 35-45 minutes, stirring occasionally.

5 Meanwhile, slice the remaining onion. Heat the remaining oil in a pan and fry the onion until golden. Set aside.

6 Once the meat is tender, add the *aamchoor* (dried mango powder), the remaining green chilli and fresh coriander (cilantro) leaves and stir-fry for 3-5 minutes.

7 Transfer the curry to a serving dish and pour the fried onion slices and oil along the centre. Serve hot with rice.

Lamb Pot Roast

Serves 6

INGREDIENTS

2.5 kg/5 lb 8 oz leg of lamb	2 tsp black cumin seeds	1 large onion, peeled
2 tsp fresh ginger root, finely chopped	4 black peppercorns	about 2 litres/4 pints/10 cups water
2 tsp fresh garlic, crushed	3 cloves	
2 tsp garam masala	1 tsp chilli powder	
1 tsp salt	3 tbsp lemon juice	
	300 ml/$\frac{1}{2}$ pint/1$\frac{1}{4}$ cups oil	

1 Remove the fat from the lamb with a sharp knife. Prick the lamb all over with a fork.

2 In a bowl, mix the ginger, garlic, garam masala, salt, black cumin seeds, peppercorns, cloves and chilli powder until well combined. Stir in the lemon juice and mix well. Then spoon the mixture over the leg of lamb and rub into the meat, making sure it is well coated, and set aside.

3 Heat the oil in a pan. Add the meat to the pan and place the onion alongside the leg of lamb.

4 Add enough water to cover the meat and cook over a low heat for 2$\frac{1}{2}$-3 hours, turning occasionally. (If after a while the water has evaporated and the meat is not tender, add a little extra water.) Once the water has completely evaporated, turn the roast over to brown it on all sides.

5 Remove the roast from the pan and transfer to a serving dish. Cut the roast into slices or serve it whole to be carved at the table. Serve the lamb hot or cold.

COOK'S TIP

Traditionally, a pan called a degchi is used for pot-roasting in India. It is set over hot ashes and contains hot coals in its lid.

Grilled Minced Lamb

Serves 4

INGREDIENTS

5 tbsp oil	1 tsp fresh garlic, crushed	salad leaves, to serve
2 onions, sliced	1 tsp salt	
450 g/1 lb minced lamb	1$\frac{1}{2}$ tsp garam masala	TO GARNISH:
2 tbsp yogurt	$\frac{1}{2}$ tsp ground allspice	fresh coriander (cilantro)
1 tsp chilli powder	2 fresh green chillies	leaves, chopped
1 tsp fresh ginger root, finely	fresh coriander (cilantro)	1 lemon, cut into wedges
chopped	leaves	

1 Heat the oil in a saucepan. Add the sliced onions and fry until golden brown.

2 Place the minced lamb in a large bowl. Add the yogurt, chilli powder, ginger, garlic, salt, garam masala, ground allspice and mix to combine.

3 Add the lamb mixture to the fried onions and stir-fry for 10-15 minutes. Remove the mixture from the heat and set aside.

4 Meanwhile, place the green chillies and half of the coriander (cilantro) leaves in a processor and grind. Alternatively, finely chop the green chillies and coriander (cilantro) with a sharp knife. Set aside until required.

5 Put the minced lamb mixture in a food processor and grind. Alternatively, place in a large bowl and mash with a fork. Mix the lamb mixture with the chillies and coriander (cilantro) and blend well.

6 Transfer the mixture to a shallow heatproof dish. Cook under a preheated medium-hot grill (broiler) for 10-15 minutes, moving the mixture about with a fork. Watch it carefully to prevent it from burning.

7 Garnish with coriander (cilantro) leaves and lemon wedges, and serve with salad leaves.

Minced Lamb with Peas

Serves 4

INGREDIENTS

6 tbsp oil	2 tomatoes, chopped	1 tsp chilli powder
1 medium onion, sliced	1 tsp salt	450 g/1 lb lean minced lamb
3 green chillies	1 tsp fresh ginger root, finely	100 g/3^1/2 oz peas
fresh coriander (cilantro)	chopped	
leaves	1 tsp fresh garlic, crushed	

1 Heat the oil in a medium-sized saucepan. Add the onion slices and fry until golden brown, stirring.

2 Add two of the green chillies, half of the fresh coriander (cilantro) leaves and the chopped tomatoes to the pan and reduce the heat to a gentle simmer.

3 Add the salt, ginger, garlic and chilli powder to the mixture in the pan and stir everything well to combine.

4 Add the minced lamb to the pan and stir-fry the mixture for 7-10 minutes, until the meat turns brown.

5 Add the peas to the mixture in the pan and cook for a further 3-4 minutes, stirring occasionally.

6 Transfer the lamb and pea mixture to warm serving plates and garnish with the remaining chopped green chilli and the fresh coriander (cilantro) leaves.

COOK'S TIP

The flavour of garlic can be changed according to how it is prepared. For instance, a whole garlic clove added to a dish will give it the flavour but not the 'bite' of garlic; a halved clove will add a little bite while a finely chopped garlic clove will release most of the flavour and a crushed clove will release all of the flavour.

Lamb Curry in a Thick Sauce

Serves 6

INGREDIENTS

1 kg/2 lb 4 oz lean lamb, with or without bone	2 tsp fresh garlic, crushed	3 green chillies, chopped
7 tbsp yogurt	$1^1/_2$ tsp chilli powder	2 tbsp lemon juice
75 g/$2^3/_4$ oz/5 tbsp almonds	$1^1/_2$ tsp salt	400 g/14 oz can tomatoes
2 tsp garam masala	300 ml/$^1/_2$ pint/$1^1/_4$ cups oil	300 ml/$^1/_2$ pint/$1^1/_4$ cups water
2 tsp fresh ginger root, finely chopped	3 onions, finely chopped	fresh coriander (cilantro) leaves, chopped
	4 green cardamoms	
	2 bay leaves	

1 Using a sharp knife, cut the lamb into small, even-sized pieces.

2 In a large mixing bowl, combine the yogurt, almonds, garam masala, ginger, garlic, chilli powder and salt, stirring well to mix the ingredients well.

3 Heat the oil in a large saucepan and fry the onions with the cardamoms and the bay leaves until golden brown, stirring constantly.

4 Add the meat and the yogurt mixture to the pan and stir-fry for 3-5 minutes.

5 Add 2 of the chopped green chillies, the lemon juice and the canned tomatoes to the mixture in the pan and stir-fry for a further 5 minutes.

6 Add the water to the pan. Then cover the curry and leave to simmer gently over a low heat for 35-40 minutes.

7 Add the remaining green chilli and the coriander (cilantro) leaves and stir until the sauce has thickened. (Remove the lid and turn the heat higher if the sauce is too watery.)

8 Transfer the curry to warm serving plates and serve hot.

Potatoes Cooked with Meat & Yogurt

Serves 6

INGREDIENTS

300 ml/½ pint/1¼ cups oil
3 medium onions, sliced
1 kg/2 lb 4 oz leg of lamb,
    cubed with or without
    bone
2 tsp garam masala
1½ tsp fresh ginger root,
    finely chopped
1½ tsp fresh garlic, crushed

1 tsp chilli powder
3 black peppercorns
3 green cardamoms
1 tsp black cumin seeds
2 cinnamon sticks
1 tsp paprika
1½ tsp salt
150 ml/5 fl oz/²/3 cup natural
    yogurt

600 ml/1 pint/2½ cups water
3 medium potatoes

TO GARNISH:
2 green chillies, chopped
fresh coriander (cilantro)
    leaves, chopped

1 Heat the oil in a saucepan and fry the sliced onions until golden brown. Remove the onions from the pan and set aside.

2 Add the meat to the saucepan with 5 ml/ 1 tsp of the garam masala and stir-fry for 5-7 minutes over a low heat.

3 Add the onions to the pan and remove from the heat.

4 Meanwhile in a small bowl, mix together the ginger, garlic, chilli powder, peppercorns, cardamoms, cumin seeds, cinnamon sticks, paprika and salt. Add the yogurt and mix well.

5 Return the pan to the heat and gradually add the spice and yogurt mixture to the meat and onions and stir-fry for 7-10 minutes. Add the water, lower the heat and cook, covered, for about 40 minutes, stirring the mixture occasionally.

6 Peel and cut the potatoes into 6 pieces, then add them to the pan and cook, covered, for a further 15 minutes, gently stirring the mixture occasionally. Garnish the curry with green chillies and fresh coriander (cilantro) leaves, and serve at once.

Lean Lamb Cooked in Spinach

Serves 2–4

INGREDIENTS

300 ml/$\frac{1}{2}$ pint/1$\frac{1}{4}$ cups oil
2 medium onions, sliced
$\frac{1}{4}$ bunch fresh coriander
   (cilantro)
3 green chillies, chopped
1$\frac{1}{2}$ tsp fresh ginger root,
   finely chopped
1$\frac{1}{2}$ tsp fresh garlic, crushed
1 tsp chilli powder

$\frac{1}{2}$ tsp turmeric
450 g/1 lb lean lamb, with or
   without the bone
1 tsp salt
1 kg/2 lb 4 oz fresh spinach,
   trimmed, washed and
   chopped or 425g/
   15 oz can spinach

700 ml/1$\frac{1}{4}$ pints/3$\frac{1}{4}$ cups
   water

TO GARNISH:
fresh red chillies, finely
   chopped

1 Heat the oil in a saucepan and fry the onions until they turn a pale colour.

2 Add the fresh coriander (cilantro) and 2 of the chopped green chillies to the pan and stir-fry for 3-5 minutes.

3 Reduce the heat and add the ginger, garlic, chilli powder and turmeric to the pan, stirring to mix.

4 Add the lamb to the pan and stir-fry for a further 5 minutes. Add the salt and the fresh or canned spinach and cook, stirring occasionally with a wooden spoon, for a further 3-5 minutes.

5 Add the water, stirring, and cook over a low heat, covered, for about 45 minutes. Remove the lid and check the meat. If it is not tender, turn the meat over, increase the heat and cook, uncovered, until the surplus water has been absorbed. Stir-fry the mixture for a further 5-7 minutes.

6 Transfer the lamb and spinach mixture to a serving dish and garnish with finely chopped red chillies. Serve hot.

Spicy Lamb Chops

Serves 4-6

INGREDIENTS

1 kg/2 lb 4 oz lamb chops	1 tsp black cumin seeds	TO GARNISH:
2 tsp fresh ginger root, finely chopped	1½ tsp salt	fried potato chips
	850 ml/1½ pints/3¾ cups water	tomatoes
2 tsp fresh garlic, crushed		lemon wedges
1 tsp pepper	2 medium eggs	fresh coriander (cilantro) sprigs
1 tsp garam masala	300 ml/½ pint/1½ cups oil	

1 Using a sharp knife, trim away any excess fat from the lamb chops.

2 Mix the ginger, garlic, pepper, garam masala, cumin seeds and salt together and rub all over the chops.

3 Bring the water to a boil, add the chops and spice mixture and cook for about 45 minutes, stirring occasionally. Once the water has evaporated, remove from the heat and set aside to cool.

4 Using a fork, beat the eggs together in a bowl.

5 Heat the oil in a large saucepan.

6 Dip each lamb chop into the beaten egg and then fry them in the saucepan for 3 minutes, turning each once.

7 Transfer the chops to a serving dish and garnish with fried potato chips, tomatoes, lemon wedges and coriander (cilantro). Serve hot.

COOK'S TIP

Garam masala is a mixture of ground spices, not an individual spice. The usual combination includes cardamom, cinnamon, cloves, cumin, nutmeg and black peppercorns, but most Indian cooks have a personal recipe, often handed down for generations. You can buy prepared garam masala at large supermarkets or Asian grocery stores.

Stuffed Tomatoes

Serves 4-6

INGREDIENTS

6 large, firm tomatoes
50 g/1^3/$_4$ oz/4 tbsp unsalted
    butter
1 medium onion, finely
    chopped
5 tbsp oil

1 tsp fresh ginger root, finely
    chopped
1 tsp fresh garlic, crushed
1 tsp pepper
1 tsp salt
^{1}/$_2$ tsp garam masala

450 g/1 lb minced lamb
1 green chilli
fresh coriander (cilantro)
    leaves

---

1 Preheat the oven to 180°C/ 350°F/Gas Mark 4. Rinse the tomatoes, cut off the tops and scoop out the flesh.

2 Grease a heatproof dish with 50 g/1^3/$_4$ oz/ 4 tbsp butter. Place the tomatoes in the dish.

3 Heat the oil in a pan and fry the onion until golden brown.

4 Lower the heat and add the ginger, garlic, pepper, salt and garam masala. Stir-fry the mixture for 3-5 minutes.

5 Add the minced lamb to the saucepan and fry for 10-15 minutes.

6 Add the green chilli and fresh coriander (cilantro) leaves and continue stir-frying the mixture for 3-5 minutes.

7 Spoon the lamb mixture into the tomatoes and replace the tops. Cook the tomatoes in the oven for 15-20 minutes.

8 Transfer the tomatoes to serving plates and serve hot.

VARIATION

You could use the same recipe to stuff red or green (bell) peppers, if you prefer.

Cubed Lamb Kebabs (Kabobs)

Serves 6-8

INGREDIENTS

1 kg/2 lb 4 oz lean lamb,
  boned and cubed
1 tsp meat tenderizer
1½ tsp fresh ginger root,
  finely chopped
1½ tsp fresh garlic, crushed
1 tsp chilli powder

½ tsp turmeric
½ tsp salt
2 tbsp water
8 tomatoes, cut in half
8 small pickling onions
10 mushrooms

1 green (bell) pepper, cut into
  large pieces
1 red (bell) pepper, cut into
  large pieces
2 tbsp oil
2 lemons, cut into quarters, to
  garnish

1 Wash the cubed lamb and place it in a clean dish. Apply the tenderizer to the meat, using your hands. Then set the dish aside for about 3 hours at room temperature.

2 Mix together the ginger, garlic, chilli powder, turmeric and salt in a bowl. Add the water and mix with the spices to form a paste. Add the cubed meat and mix until it is well coated with the spice mixture.

3 Arrange the meat cubes on skewers, alternating with the tomatoes, pickling onions, mushrooms and (bell) peppers. Brush the meat and vegetables with the oil.

4 Grill (broil) the kebabs (kabobs) under a pre-heated grill (broiler) for 25-30 minutes or until the meat is cooked through. When cooked, remove the kebabs (kabobs) from the grill (broiler) and transfer to a serving plate. Arrange lemon wedges on the side and serve immediately with boiled rice and a Raita (see page 216).

COOK'S TIP

If using wooden skewers, soak them in cold water for 20 minutes before they are used to prevent them from burning during cooking.

Cauliflower with Meat

Serves 4

INGREDIENTS

1 medium cauliflower
2 green chillies
300 ml/$\frac{1}{2}$ pint/$1\frac{1}{4}$ cups oil
2 onions, sliced
450 g/1 lb cubed lamb
1$\frac{1}{2}$ tsp fresh ginger root,
   finely chopped

1$\frac{1}{2}$ tsp fresh garlic, crushed
1 tsp chilli powder
1 tsp salt
fresh coriander (cilantro)
   leaves, chopped
850 ml/1$\frac{1}{2}$ pints/3$\frac{3}{4}$ cups
   water

1 tbsp lemon juice

BAGHAAR:
150 ml/$\frac{1}{4}$ pint/$\frac{2}{3}$ cup oil
4 dried red chillies
1 tsp mixed mustard and
   onion seeds

---

1 Using a sharp knife, cut the cauliflower into small florets. Chop the green chillies finely.

2 Heat the oil in a large saucepan. Add the onions and fry until golden brown.

3 Reduce the heat and add the meat, stirring.

4 Add the ginger, garlic, chilli powder and salt. Stir-fry for about 5 minutes, stirring to mix.

5 Add 1 green chilli and half of the coriander (cilantro) leaves.

6 Stir in the water and cook, covered, over a low heat for about 30 minutes.

7 Add the cauliflower and simmer for a further 15-20 minutes or until the water has totally evaporated. Stir-fry for another 5 minutes. Remove from the heat and sprinkle the lemon juice sparingly.

8 To make the *baghaar*, heat the oil in a separate small saucepan. Add the dried red chillies and the mixed mustard and onion seeds and fry until they turn a darker colour, stirring occasionally. Remove the pan from the heat and pour the mixture over the cooked cauliflower.

9 Garnish with the remaining green chilli and fresh coriander (cilantro). Serve at once.

Lamb & Lentils

Serves 6

INGREDIENTS

100 g/3¹/₂ oz/¹/₂ cup
    chana dhaal
100 g/3¹/₂ oz/¹/₂ cup
    masoor dhaal
100 g/3¹/₂ oz/¹/₂ cup
    moong dhaal
100 g/3¹/₂ oz/¹/₂ cup
    urid dhaal
75 g/2³/₄ oz/5 tbsp
    porridge oats

KHORMA:
1.5 kg/3 lb 5 oz lamb, cubed
    with bones

200 ml/7 fl oz/³/₄ cup yogurt
2 tsp fresh ginger root, finely
    chopped
2 tsp fresh garlic, crushed
1 tbsp garam masala
2 tsp chilli powder
¹/₂ tsp turmeric
3 whole green cardamoms
2 cinnamon sticks
1 tsp black cumin seeds
2 tsp salt
450 ml/16 fl oz/2 cups oil
5 medium onions, sliced

700 ml/1¹/₄ pints/3¹/₄ cups
    water
2 green chillies, chopped
fresh coriander (cilantro)
    leaves

TO GARNISH:
6 green chillies, chopped
¹/₂ bunch fresh coriander
    (cilantro) leaves, chopped
2 pieces fresh ginger root,
    shredded
3 lemons, cut into wedges

1 Soak the *dhaals* and oats overnight. Boil in a pan of water until soft. Mash and set aside.

2 Mix the lamb with the yogurt, spices and salt

3 Heat 300 ml/¹/₂ pint/1¹/₄ cups of the oil in a pan and fry 4 of the onions until golden. Add the meat and stir-fry for 7-10 minutes. Stir in the water, lower the heat and cook, covered, for 1 hour.

4 Stir the *dhaals* into the meat. If it is too thick, add 300 ml/¹/₂ pint/

1¹/₄ cups water, and cook for 10-12 minutes. Add the chillies and the coriander (cilantro). Transfer to a serving dish.

5 Fry the remaining onion and pour over the lamb and lentils. Garnish and serve.

Meatballs in Sauce

Serves 4

INGREDIENTS

450 g/1 lb minced lamb
1 tsp fresh ginger root, crushed
1 tsp fresh garlic, crushed
1 tsp garam masala
1 1/2 tsp poppy seeds
1 tsp salt
1/2 tsp chilli powder
1 medium onion, finely chopped
1 green chilli, finely chopped

fresh coriander (cilantro) leaves
1 tbsp gram flour
150 ml/1/4 pint/2/3 cup oil

SAUCE:
2 tbsp oil
3 medium onions, finely chopped
2 small cinnamon sticks
2 large black cardamoms

1 tsp fresh ginger root, finely chopped
1 tsp fresh garlic, crushed
1 tsp salt
75 ml/3 fl oz/41/2 tbsp natural yogurt
150 ml/1/4 pint/2/3 cup water

TO GARNISH:
fresh coriander (cilantro) leaves, finely chopped
1 green chilli, finely chopped

1 Place the lamb in a large mixing bowl. Add the ginger, garlic, garam masala, poppy seeds, salt, chilli powder, onion, chilli, coriander (cilantro) and gram flour and mix well with a fork.

2 Make small meatballs out of the mixture with your hands; set aside.

3 To make the sauce, heat the oil and fry the onions until golden brown. Add the cinnamon sticks and cardamoms to the pan, lower the heat and stir-fry for a further 5 minutes. Add the ginger, garlic, salt, yogurt and water; mix well.

4 Transfer to a serving bowl and garnish with chopped coriander (cilantro) and chillies.

5 Heat the oil and fry the meatballs for 8-10 minutes or until golden brown.

6 Transfer the meatballs to warm plates. Serve with the sauce and Chapatis (see page 180).

Sheekh Kebabs (Kabobs)

Makes 10-12

INGREDIENTS

2 tsp meat tenderizer
450 g/1 lb lean minced lamb
fresh coriander (cilantro)
    leaves
1 medium onion, finely
    chopped
2 green chillies, finely chopped

2 tbsp yogurt
1 tsp fresh ginger root, finely
    chopped
1 tsp fresh garlic, crushed
1 tsp ground cumin
1 tsp ground coriander
1/2 tsp salt

1 tsp chilli powder
1/2 tsp ground allspice
1 tsp garam masala
chilli powder and fresh
    coriander (cilantro), to
    garnish
lemon wedges, to serve

1 Apply the meat tenderizer to the minced lamb with your fingers and blend in well. Set aside for at least 3 hours.

2 Meanwhile, chop the coriander (cilantro) finely. Mix the onion, green chillies and coriander (cilantro) in a bowl.

3 In a separate bowl, mix the yogurt with the ginger, garlic, ground cumin, ground coriander, salt, chilli powder, ground allspice and garam masala. Then blend this with the onion mixture.

4 Blend the combined mixture into the minced lamb and mix together with your hands. Divide the mixture into 10-12 equal portions. Roll each portion around a skewer with your fingers, gently pressing all around.

5 Grill (broil) the lamb kebabs (kabobs) under a medium grill (broiler), basting with the oil.

6 Garnish with chilli powder and coriander (cilantro) and serve with lemon wedges and a Raita (see page 216).

VARIATION

These kababs (kabobs) are delicious cooked over a barbecue (grill). Serve in pitta bread for a party dish or add the meat to a salad.

Spicy Lamb Curry in Sauce

Serves 4

INGREDIENTS

2 tsp ground cumin	1 tsp fresh ginger root, finely	3 medium onions, sliced
2 tsp ground coriander	chopped	850 ml/1½ pints/3¾ cups
2 tsp desiccated (shredded)	1 tsp fresh garlic, crushed	water
coconut	1 tsp chilli powder	2 tbsp lemon juice
1 tsp mixed mustard and	1 tsp salt	4 green chillies, split
onion seeds	450 g/1 lb lean lamb, cubed	
2 tsp sesame seeds	450 ml/16 fl oz/2 cups oil	

1 Dry roast the ground cumin, ground coriander, desiccated (shredded) coconut, mixed mustard and onion seeds and the sesame seeds in a heavy frying pan (skillet), shaking the pan frequently to stop the spices from burning. Then grind the roasted spices using a pestle and mortar.

2 In a large mixing bowl, blend together the roasted ground spices along with the ginger, garlic, chilli powder, salt and the cubed lamb and set aside.

3 In a separate pan, heat 300 ml/½ pint/1½ cups of oil and fry the onions until golden brown.

4 Add the meat mixture to the onions and stir-fry for 5–7 minutes over a low heat. Add the water and simmer for 45 minutes, stirring occasionally. When the meat is cooked through, remove from the heat and sprinkle with lemon juice.

5 In a separate saucepan, heat the remaining oil and add the four split green chillies. Reduce the heat and cover with a lid. Remove the pan from the heat after about 30 seconds and set aside to cool.

6 Pour the chilli oil mixture over the meat curry and serve hot with Onion Dhaal (see page 142) and plain boiled rice.

Meat-Coated Eggs

Serves 6

INGREDIENTS

450 g/1 lb lean minced lamb
1 small onion, finely chopped
1 green chilli, finely chopped
1 tsp fresh ginger root, finely
    chopped

1 tsp fresh garlic, crushed
1 tsp ground coriander
1 tsp garam masala
1 tsp salt
1½ tbsp gram flour

7 eggs, 6 of them hard-boiled
    (hard-cooked) and shelled,
    1 beaten
oil, for deep-frying

1 Place the lamb, onion and the green chilli in a bowl and mix together. Transfer the mixture to a food processor and work until well ground. (Alternatively, grind the mixture by hand using a pestle and mortar).

2 Remove the mixture from the food processor and add the ginger, garlic, ground coriander, garam masala, salt, gram flour and the beaten egg. Combine all the ingredients together with your hands.

3 Divide the mixture into 6 equal portions. Roll each portion out to form a flat round, about 5 mm/¼ inch thick. Place a hard-boiled (hard-cooked) egg in the middle of each round and wrap the meat mixture around the egg to enclose it completely. When all 6 eggs have been covered, set aside in a cool place for 20-30 minutes.

4 Meanwhile, heat the oil in a *karahi* or deep frying pan (skillet). Gently drop the meat-coated eggs into the oil and fry for 2-4 minutes or until golden brown. Using a perforated spoon, remove the meat-coated eggs from the oil, transfer to kitchen paper and drain thoroughly. Serve hot.

VARIATION

If you wish to serve these Meat-Coated Eggs in a sauce, use the recipe for Meatballs in Sauce (see page 36).

Chicken & Mushroom Curry

Serves 4

INGREDIENTS

4-6 chicken breasts
3 tbsp vegetable oil
2 onions, sliced
2 garlic cloves, crushed
2.5 cm/1 inch piece ginger
   root, chopped finely
2 fresh green chillies, seeded
   and chopped, or use
   1-2 tsp minced chilli (from
   a jar)
1 1/2 tbsp medium curry paste

1 tsp ground coriander
175-250 g/6-9 oz mushrooms,
   sliced thickly
850 ml/1 1/2 pints/3 1/2 cups
   stock
3 tomatoes, chopped
1/2-1 tsp salt
60 g/2 oz creamed coconut,
   chopped
2 tbsp ground almonds

TO GARNISH:
2 tbsp vegetable oil
1 green or red (bell) pepper,
   seeded and cut into thin
   strips
6 spring onions (scallions),
   trimmed and sliced
1 tsp cumin seeds

1 Cut the chicken into small bite-sized pieces. Heat the oil in a saucepan, and fry the chicken until sealed, stirring frequently. Remove the chicken from the pan.

2 Add the onions, garlic, ginger, chillies, curry paste and ground coriander to the saucepan and cook gently for 2 minutes, Stir in the mushrooms, stock and tomatoes, and season with a little salt.

3 Return the chicken to the pan, then cover and simmer very gently for 1 1/4-1 1/2 hours or until the chicken is tender.

4 Stir the creamed coconut and ground almonds into the curry, then cover the pan and cook gently for 3 minutes.

5 Meanwhile, make the garnish. Heat the oil in a frying pan (skillet), add the (bell) pepper strips and spring onion (scallion) slices and fry gently until glistening and tender-crisp. Stir in the cumin seeds and fry for 30 seconds. Spoon over the curry and serve.

Beef Kebabs (Kabobs)

Makes 10-12

INGREDIENTS

3 tbsp *chana dhaal*
450 g/1 lb lean beef, boned
    and cubed
1 tsp fresh ginger root, finely
    chopped
1 tsp fresh garlic, crushed
1 tsp chilli powder
1½ tsp salt

1½ tsp garam masala
3 green chillies
fresh coriander (cilantro)
    leaves
1 medium onion, chopped
300 ml/½ pint/1¼ cups oil
850 ml/1½ pints/3½ cups
    water

2 tbsp natural yogurt
1 medium egg

TO GARNISH:
onion rings
lemon wedges

1 Rinse the *chana dhaal* twice, removing any stones or other impurities. Boil the *chana dhaal* in a pan of water until the water dries up and the *chana dhaal* has softened. Place in a food processor and mash to form a paste.

2 Mix the meat, ginger, garlic, chilli powder, salt and garam masala in a bowl. Add 2 green chillies, half the fresh coriander (cilantro) and the onion.

3 Heat 2 tbsp of the oil in a saucepan. Add the meat mixture to the pan. Add the water and cook, covered, over a low heat for 45-60 minutes. Once the meat is tender, evaporate any excess water by removing the lid and cooking for 10-15 minutes. Place the meat in a food processor and mash.

4 Place the yogurt, egg, mashed *chana dhaal* paste, the remaining green chilli and the coriander (cilantro) in a bowl and mix together with your fingers. Break off small balls of the meat paste and make about 12 small, flat circular shapes with the palms of your hands.

5 Heat the remaining oil in a frying pan (skillet) and cook the rounds, in batches of 3, turning once.

6 Garnish and serve immediately.

Sliced Beef with Yogurt & Spices

Serves 4

INGREDIENTS

450 g/1 lb lean beef slices, cut into 2.5 cm/1-inch slices	1 tsp salt	300 ml/^{1}/2 pint/1^1/4 cups oil
5 tbsp yogurt	2 cardamoms	2 medium onions, finely chopped
1 tsp fresh ginger root, finely chopped	1 tsp black cumin seeds	300 ml/^{1}/2 pint/1^1/4 cups water
1 tsp fresh garlic, crushed	50 g/1^3/4 oz/^{1}/4 cup ground almonds	2 red chillies, finely chopped
1 tsp chilli powder	1 tbsp desiccated (shredded) coconut	a few fresh coriander (cilantro) leaves, chopped, and red chilli strips, to garnish
1 pinch turmeric	1 tbsp poppy seeds	
2 tsp garam masala	1 tbsp sesame seeds	

1 Place the beef in a large bowl, mix with the yogurt, ginger, garlic, chilli powder, turmeric, garam masala, salt, cardamoms and black cumin seeds and set aside until required.

2 Dry roast the ground almonds, desiccated (shredded) coconut, poppy seeds and sesame seeds in a large pan until golden, shaking the pan frequently to stop the spices from burning.

3 Work the spice mixture in a food processor until finely ground. Return the mixture to the pan and add 1 tbsp of water to blend. Add the ground spice mixture to the meat mixture and combine.

4 Heat a little oil in a large saucepan and fry the onions until golden brown. Remove the onions from the pan. Stir-fry the meat in the remaining oil for about 5 minutes, then return the onions to the pan and stir-fry for a further 5-7 minutes. Add the water and simmer over a low heat, covered, for 25-30 minutes, stirring occasionally. Garnish with the coriander (cilantro) leaves and red chilli strips, and serve hot.

Beef Khorma with Almonds

Serves 6

INGREDIENTS

300 ml/^{1}/$_2$ pint/1^1/$_4$ cups oil
3 medium onions, finely
    chopped
1 kg/2 lb 4 oz lean beef, cubed
1^1/$_2$ tsp garam masala
1^1/$_2$ tsp ground coriander
1^1/$_2$ tsp fresh ginger root,
    finely chopped

1^1/$_2$ tsp fresh garlic, crushed
1 tsp salt
150 ml/5 fl oz/^{2}/$_3$ cup natural
    yogurt
2 cloves
3 green cardamoms
4 black peppercorns
600 ml/1 pint/2^1/$_2$ cups water

TO GARNISH:
6 almonds, soaked, peeled and
    chopped
2 green chillies, chopped
a few fresh coriander
    (cilantro) leaves

1 Heat the oil in a saucepan. Add the onions and stir-fry until golden brown.

2 Add the meat to the onions in the pan and stir-fry for about 5 minutes. Remove the pan from the heat.

3 Mix the garam masala, ground coriander, ginger, garlic, salt and yogurt in a bowl. Gradually add the meat to the yogurt and spice mixture and mix to coat the meat on all sides. Place in the saucepan, return to the heat, and stir-fry for 5-7 minutes, or until the mixture is nearly brown in colour.

4 Add the cloves, green cardamoms and black peppercorns. Add the water, lower the heat, cover and leave to simmer for about 45-60 minutes. If the water has completely evaporated but the meat is still not tender enough, add another 300 ml/ ^{1}/$_2$ pint/1^1/$_2$ cups water and cook for a further 10-15 minutes, stirring occasionally.

5 Just before serving, garnish with chopped almonds, green chillies and the fresh coriander (cilantro) leaves. Serve with Chapatis (see page 180).

Beef Cooked in Whole Spices

Serves 4

INGREDIENTS

300 ml/^{1}/2 pint/1^1/4 cups oil
3 medium onions, chopped
  finely
2.5 cm/1 inch ginger root,
  shredded
4 cloves garlic, shredded

2 cinnamon sticks
3 whole green cardamoms
3 whole cloves
4 whole black peppercorns
6 dried red chillies, chopped
150 ml/5 fl oz/^{2}/3 cup yogurt

450 g/1 lb beef, with or
  without bone, cut into
  cubes
3 green chillies, chopped
600 ml/1 pint/2^1/2 cups water
fresh coriander (cilantro)
  leaves

1 Heat the oil in a frying pan (skillet) and fry the onions, stirring, until golden brown.

2 Reduce the heat and add the ginger, garlic, cinnamon sticks, green cardamoms, cloves, black peppercorns and red chillies to the pan and stir-fry for 5 minutes.

3 In a bowl, whip the yogurt with a fork. Add the yogurt to the onions and stir to combine.

4 Add the meat and 2 of the green chillies to the frying pan (skillet) and stir-fry the mixture for 5-7 minutes.

5 Gradually add the water to the pan, stirring well. Cover the pan and cook the beef and spice mixture for 1 hour, stirring and adding more water if necessary.

6 When thoroughly cooked through, remove the pan from the heat and transfer the beef and spice mixture to a serving dish. Garnish with the remaining chopped green chilli and the fresh coriander (cilantro) leaves.

VARIATION

Substitute lamb for the beef in this recipe, if you prefer.

Fried Kidneys

Serves 4

INGREDIENTS

450 g/1 lb lamb's kidneys
2 tsp turmeric
2¹/₂ tsp salt
150 ml/¹/₄ pint/²/₃ cup water

1 green (bell) pepper, sliced
1 tsp fresh ginger root, finely
   chopped
1 tsp fresh garlic, crushed

1 tsp chilli powder
3 tbsp oil
1 small onion, finely chopped
coriander (cilantro) leaves, to
   garnish

1 Using a sharp knife, remove the very fine skin surrounding each kidney. Cut each kidney into 4-6 pieces.

2 Place the kidney pieces in a bowl with the turmeric and 2 teaspoons of salt. Pour in the water, mix with a spoon to combine the ingredients and leave to marinate for about 1 hour. Drain the kidney pieces thoroughly and discard the marinade, then rinse them under cold running water until the water runs completely clear.

3 Place the kidneys in a small saucepan together with the green (bell) pepper. Pour in enough water to cover and cook over a medium heat, leaving the lid of the pan slightly ajar so that the steam can escape, until all of the water has evaporated.

4 Add the ginger, garlic, chilli powder and remaining salt to the kidney mixture and blend until well combined.

5 Add the oil, onion and the coriander (cilantro) to the pan, and stir-fry for 7-10 minutes.

6 Transfer the kidneys to a serving plate and serve hot.

COOK'S TIP

Many people are resistant to the idea of cooking or eating kidneys because they often have rather a strong smell – even when cooked. However, if you wash and soak them in water, you can largely avoid this problem.

Chicken Tikka

Serves 6

INGREDIENTS

1 tsp fresh ginger root, finely chopped	1 tsp salt	3 tbsp oil
1 tsp fresh garlic, crushed	2 tbsp lemon juice	
1/2 tsp ground coriander	a few drops of red food colouring (optional)	TO GARNISH:
1/2 tsp ground cumin	1 tbsp tomato purée (paste)	6 lettuce leaves
1 tsp chilli powder	1.5 kg/3 lb 5 oz chicken breast	1 lemon, cut into wedges
3 tbsp yogurt	1 onion, sliced	

1 Blend together the ginger, garlic, ground coriander, ground cumin and chilli powder in a large mixing bowl.

2 Add the yogurt, salt, lemon juice, red food colouring (if using) and the tomato purée (paste) to the spice mixture.

3 Using a sharp knife, cut the chicken into pieces. Add the chicken to the spice mixture and toss to coat well. Leave to marinate for 3 hours, or preferably overnight.

4 Arrange the onion in the bottom of a heatproof dish. Carefully drizzle half of the oil over the onions.

5 Arrange the marinated chicken pieces on top of the onions and cook them under a pre-heated grill (broiler), turning each piece once and basting with the remaining oil, for 25-30 minutes.

6 Serve the chicken tikka on a bed of lettuce and garnish with the lemon wedges.

COOK'S TIP

Chicken Tikka can be served with Naan Breads (see page 178), Raita (see page 216) and Mango Chutney (see page 218) or as a starter.

Chicken Tossed in Black Pepper

Serves 4-6

INGREDIENTS

8 chicken thighs
1 tsp fresh ginger root, finely
    chopped
1 tsp fresh garlic, crushed
1 tsp salt
1 1/2 tsp pepper
150 ml/1/4 pint/2/3 cup oil

1 green (bell) pepper, roughly
    sliced
150 ml/1/4 pint/2/3 cup water
2 tbsp lemon juice

FRIED CORN & PEAS:
50 g/2 oz unsalted butter
200 g/8 oz frozen sweetcorn

200 g/8 oz frozen peas
1/2 tsp salt
1/2 tsp chilli powder
1 tbsp lemon juice
fresh coriander (cilantro)
    leaves, to garnish

1 Using a sharp knife, bone the chicken thighs, if you prefer.

2 Combine the ginger, garlic, salt and coarsely ground black pepper together in a mixing bowl.

3 Add the chicken pieces to the black pepper mixture and set aside.

4 Heat the oil in a large pan. Add the chicken and fry for 10 minutes.

5 Reduce the heat and add the green (bell) pepper and the water to the pan. Leave the mixture to simmer for 10 minutes, then sprinkle over the lemon juice.

6 Meanwhile, make the fried corn and peas. Melt the butter in a large frying pan (skillet). Add the frozen sweetcorn and peas and stir-fry, stirring occasionally, for about 10 minutes. Add the salt and

chilli powder and fry for a further 5 minutes.

7 Sprinkle over the lemon juice and garnish with fresh coriander (cilantro) leaves.

8 Transfer the chicken and (bell) pepper mixture to serving plates and serve with the fried corn and peas.

Chicken Kebabs (Kabobs)

Serves 6-8

INGREDIENTS

1.5 kg/3 lb 5 oz chicken, boned
1/2 tsp ground cumin
4 cardamom seeds, crushed
1/2 tsp ground cinnamon
1 tsp salt
1 tsp fresh ginger root, finely
    chopped

1 tsp fresh garlic, crushed
1/2 tsp ground allspice
1/2 tsp pepper
300 ml/1/2 pint/11/4 cups
    water
2 tbsp yogurt
2 green chillies

1 small onion
fresh coriander (cilantro)
    leaves
1 medium egg, beaten
300 ml/1/2 pint/11/4 cups oil
green salad leaves and lemon
    wedges, to garnish

1 Place the boned chicken in a large saucepan. Add the ground cumin, cardamom seeds, ground cinnamon, salt, ginger, garlic, ground allspice and pepper and pour in the water. Bring the mixture to the boil until all of the water has been absorbed.

2 Put the mixture in a food processor and grind to form a smooth paste. Transfer the paste to a mixing bowl. Add the yogurt and blend together until well combined.

3 Place the green chillies, onion and coriander (cilantro) leaves in the food processor and grind finely. Add to the chicken mixture and mix well. Add the beaten egg and mix to combine.

4 Break 12-15 portions off from the mixture and make them into small, flat round shapes in the palm of your hand.

5 Heat the oil in a saucepan and fry the kebabs (kabobs) gently, in batches, over a low heat, turning once. Drain thoroughly on kitchen paper and serve hot.

COOK'S TIP

Indian kebab (kabob) dishes are not necessarily cooked on a skewer; they can also be served in a dish and are always dry dishes with no sauce.

Chicken & Onions

Serves 4

INGREDIENTS

300 ml/¹/2 pint/1¹/4 cups oil
4 medium onions, finely
    chopped
1¹/2 tsp fresh ginger root,
    finely chopped
1¹/2 tsp garam masala
1¹/2 tsp fresh garlic, crushed

1 tsp chilli powder
1 tsp ground coriander
3 whole cardamoms
3 peppercorns
3 tbsp tomato purée (paste)
8 chicken thighs, skinned

300 ml/¹/2 pint/1¹/4 cups
    water
2 tbsp lemon juice
1 green chilli
fresh coriander (cilantro)
    leaves
green chilli strips, to garnish

1 Heat the oil in a large frying pan (skillet). Add the onion and fry, stirring occasionally, until golden brown.

2 Reduce the heat and add the ginger, garam masala, garlic, chilli powder, ground coriander, whole cardamoms and the peppercorns, stirring well to mix.

3 Add the tomato purée (paste) to the mixture in the frying pan (skillet)

and stir-fry with the spices for 5-7 minutes.

4 Add the chicken thighs to the pan and toss in the spice mixture to coat them thoroughly

5 Pour the water into the saucepan, cover and leave the curry to simmer for 20-25 minutes.

6 Add the lemon juice, green chilli and coriander (cilantro) to the mixture, and combine.

7 Transfer the chicken and onions to warmed serving plates, garnish and serve hot.

COOK'S TIP

A dish of meat cooked with plenty of onions is called a Do Pyaza. This curry definitely improves if made in advance and then reheated before serving. This develops the flavours and makes them deeper.

Chicken Drumsticks Deep-Fried with Herbs & Spices

Serves 4

INGREDIENTS

8 chicken drumsticks
1¹/₂ tsp fresh ginger root, finely chopped
1¹/₂ tsp fresh garlic, crushed
1 tsp salt

2 medium onions, chopped
¹/₂ large bunch fresh coriander (cilantro) leaves
4-6 green chillies
600 ml/1 pint/2¹/₂ cups oil

4 firm tomatoes, cut into wedges
2 large green (bell) peppers, roughly chopped

1 Make 2-3 slashes in each piece of chicken. Rub the ginger, garlic and salt over the chicken pieces and set aside.

2 Place half of the onions, the coriander (cilantro) leaves and green chillies in a pestle and mortar and grind to a paste. Rub the paste over the chicken pieces.

3 Heat the oil in a *karahi* or large frying pan (skillet). Add the remaining onions and fry until golden brown. Remove the onions from the pan with a perforated spoon and set aside.

4 Reduce the heat to medium hot and fry the chicken pieces, in batches of about 2 at a time, until they are cooked through (about 5-7 minutes per piece).

5 When all of the chicken pieces are cooked through, remove them from the pan, keep warm and set aside.

6 Add the tomato wedges and the green (bell) peppers to the pan and half-cook them until they are softened but still have 'bite'.

7 Transfer the tomatoes and (bell) peppers to a serving plate and arrange the chicken on top. Garnish with the reserved fried onions.

Chicken Khorma

Serves 4-6

INGREDIENTS

1¹/₂ tsp fresh ginger root, finely chopped
1¹/₂ tsp fresh garlic, crushed
2 tsp garam masala
1 tsp chilli powder
1 tsp salt
1 tsp black cumin seeds

3 green cardamoms, with husks removed and seeds crushed
1 tsp ground coriander
1 tsp ground almonds
150 ml/5 fl oz/²/₃ cup natural yogurt
8 whole chicken breasts, skinned

300 ml/¹/₂ pint/1¹/₄ cups oil
2 medium onions, sliced
150 ml/¹/₄ pint/²/₃ cup water
fresh coriander (cilantro) leaves
green chillies, chopped
boiled rice, to serve

1 Mix the ginger, garlic, garam masala, chilli powder, salt, black cumin seeds, green cardamoms, ground coriander and almonds with the yogurt.

2 Spoon the yogurt and spice mixture over the chicken breasts and set aside to marinate.

3 Heat the oil in a large frying pan (skillet). Add the onions to the pan and fry until a golden brown colour.

4 Add the chicken breasts to the pan, stir-frying for 5-7 minutes.

5 Add the water, cover and leave to simmer for 20-25 minutes.

6 Add the coriander (cilantro) leaves and green chillies and cook for a further 10 minutes, stirring gently from time to time.

7 Transfer to a serving plate and serve with boiled rice.

VARIATION

Chicken portions may be used instead of breasts, if preferred, and should be cooked for 10 minutes longer in step 5.

Buttered Chicken

Serves 4-6

INGREDIENTS

100 g/3¹/2 oz/8 tbsp unsalted
  butter
1 tbsp oil
2 medium onions, finely
  chopped
1 tsp fresh ginger root, finely
  chopped
2 tsp garam masala
2 tsp ground coriander
1 tsp chilli powder

1 tsp black cumin seeds
1 tsp fresh garlic, crushed
1 tsp salt
3 whole green cardamoms
3 whole black peppercorns
150 ml/5 fl oz/²/3 cup natural
  yogurt
2 tbsp tomato purée (paste)
8 chicken pieces, skinned
150 ml/¹/4 pint/²/3 cup water

2 whole bay leaves
150 ml/5 fl oz/²/3 cup single
  (light) cream

TO GARNISH:
fresh coriander (cilantro)
  leaves
2 green chillies, chopped

1 Heat the butter and oil in a large frying pan (skillet). Add the onions and fry until golden, stirring. Reduce the heat.

2 Crush the fresh ginger and place in a bowl. Add the garam masala, ground coriander, ginger, chilli powder, black cumin seeds, garlic, salt, cardamoms and black peppercorns and blend.

Add the yogurt and tomato purée (paste) and stir to combine.

3 Add the chicken pieces to the yogurt and spice mixture and stir them to coat well.

4 Add the chicken to the onions in the pan and stir-fry vigorously, making semi-circular movements, for 5-7 minutes.

5 Add the water and the bay leaves to the mixture in the pan and leave to simmer for 30 minutes, stirring occasionally.

6 Add the cream and cook for a further 10-15 minutes.

7 Garnish with fresh coriander (cilantro) and chillies and serve hot.

Tandoori-Style Chicken

Serves 4

INGREDIENTS

8 chicken drumsticks, skinned	2 tsp ground cumin	lettuce leaves, to serve
150 ml/5 fl oz/²/₃ cup natural yogurt	2 tsp ground coriander	
	1 tsp salt	TO GARNISH:
1¹/₂ tsp fresh ginger root, finely chopped	¹/₂ tsp red food colouring	onion rings
	1 tbsp tamarind paste	sliced tomatoes
1¹/₂ tsp fresh garlic, crushed	150 ml/¹/₄ pint/²/₃ cup water	lemon wedges
1 tsp chilli powder	150 ml/¹/₄ pint/²/₃ cup oil	

1 Make 2-3 slashes in each piece of chicken.

2 Place the yogurt in a bowl. Add the ginger, garlic, chilli powder, ground cumin, ground coriander, salt and red food colouring and blend until well combined.

3 Add the chicken to the yogurt and spice mixture and mix to coat well. Leave the chicken to marinate in the refrigerator for a minimum of 3 hours.

4 In a separate bowl, mix the tamarind paste with the water and fold into the yogurt and spice mixture. Toss the chicken pieces in this mixture and set aside to marinate for a further 3 hours.

5 Transfer the chicken pieces to a heatproof dish and brush the chicken with oil. Cook the chicken under a pre-heated medium-hot grill (broiler) for 30-35 minutes, turning the chicken pieces occasionally and basting with the remaining oil.

6 Arrange the chicken on a bed of lettuce and garnish with the onion rings, tomatoes and lemon.

COOK'S TIP

Naan Bread (see page 178) and Mint Raita (see page 216) complement the dish perfectly.

Spicy Roast Chicken

Serves 4

INGREDIENTS

50 g/1³/4 oz/¹/4 cup ground almonds
50 g/1³/4 oz/¹/3 cup desiccated (shredded) coconut
150 ml/¹/4 pint/²/3 cup oil
1 medium onion, finely chopped

1 tsp fresh ginger root, chopped
1 tsp fresh garlic, crushed
1 tsp chilli powder
1¹/2 tsp garam masala
1 tsp salt
150 ml/5 fl oz/²/3 cup yogurt
4 chicken quarters, skinned

green salad leaves, to serve

TO GARNISH:
fresh coriander (cilantro) leaves
1 lemon, cut into wedges

1 In a heavy-based saucepan, dry roast the ground almonds and coconut and set aside.

2 Heat the oil in a frying pan (skillet) and fry the onion, stirring, until golden brown.

3 Place the ginger, garlic, chilli powder, garam masala and salt in a bowl and mix with the yogurt. Add the almonds and coconut and mix well.

4 Add the onions to the spice mixture, blend and set aside.

5 Arrange the chicken quarters in the bottom of a heatproof dish. Spoon the spice mixture over the chicken sparingly.

6 Cook in a pre-heated oven, 160°C/425°F/Gas Mark 3, for 35–45 minutes. Check that the chicken is cooked thoroughly by piercing the thickest part of

the meat with a sharp knife or a fine skewer – the juices will run clear when the chicken is cooked through. Garnish with the coriander (cilantro) and lemon wedges and serve with a salad.

COOK'S TIP

If you want a more spicy dish, add more chilli powder and garam masala.

Chicken Jalfrezi

Serves 4

INGREDIENTS

1 tsp mustard oil
3 tbsp vegetable oil
1 large onion, chopped finely
3 garlic cloves, crushed
1 tbsp tomato purée (paste)
2 tomatoes, peeled and
    chopped
1 tsp ground turmeric

$^1/_2$ tsp cumin seeds, ground
$^1/_2$ tsp coriander seeds, ground
$^1/_2$ tsp chilli powder
$^1/_2$ tsp garam masala
1 tsp red wine vinegar
1 small red (bell) pepper,
    chopped

125 g/4 oz/1 cup frozen broad
    (fava) beans
500 g/1 lb cooked chicken
    breasts, cut into bite-sized
    pieces
salt
fresh coriander (cilantro)
    sprigs, to garnish

1 Heat the mustard oil in a large, frying pan (skillet) set over a high heat for about 1 minute until it begins to smoke. Add the vegetable oil, reduce the heat and then add the onion and the garlic. Fry the garlic and onion until they are golden.

2 Add the tomato purée (paste), chopped tomatoes, ground turmeric, cumin and coriander seeds, chilli powder, garam masala and red wine vinegar to the frying pan (skillet). Stir the mixture until fragrant.

3 Add the red (bell) pepper and broad (fava) beans and stir for 2 minutes until the (bell) pepper is softened. Stir in the chicken, and salt to taste. Leave the curry to simmer gently for 6-8 minutes until the chicken is heated through and the beans are tender.

4 Serve garnished with coriander (cilantro).

COOK'S TIP

This dish is an ideal way of making use of leftover poultry – turkey, duck or quail. Any variety of beans works well, but vegetables are just as useful, especially root vegetables, courgettes (zucchini), potatoes or broccoli. Leafy vegetables will not be so successful.

Fried Fish in Gram Flour

Serves 4-6

INGREDIENTS

100 g/3^1/$_2$ oz/^{3}/$_4$ cup gram flour
1 tsp fresh ginger root, finely chopped
1 tsp fresh garlic, crushed
2 tsp chilli powder
1 tsp salt

^{1}/$_2$ tsp turmeric
2 fresh green chillies, chopped
fresh coriander (cilantro) leaves, chopped
300 ml/^{1}/$_2$ pint/1^1/$_4$ cups water
1 kg/2 lb 4 oz cod

300 ml/^{1}/$_2$ pint/1^1/$_4$ cups oil
cooked rice, to serve

TO GARNISH:
2 lemons, cut into wedges
6 green chillies, slit down the middle

1 Place the gram flour in a large mixing bowl. Add the ginger, garlic, chilli powder, salt and turmeric and mix to blend well.

2 Add the green chillies and the coriander (cilantro) leaves to the spiced mixture and stir to mix well.

3 Pour in the water gradually and stir thoroughly to form a semi-thick batter. Set aside until it is required.

4 Using a sharp knife, cut the cod into about 8 pieces.

5 Carefully dip the pieces of cod into the batter, coating the cod all over. Gently shake off any excess batter.

6 Heat the oil in a heavy-based frying-pan (skillet). Add the battered cod and fry, in batches, over a medium heat, turning once, until cooked through and golden.

7 Transfer the battered cod to a serving dish and garnish with lemon wedges and green chillies. Serve with cooked rice.

COOK'S TIP

Gram flour or chana dhaal flour (lentil flour) is used to make Pakoras (see page 174) and to bind kebabs (kabobs). Combined with ordinary wholemeal flour it makes a delicious Indian bread (see page 176).

Bengali-Style Fish

Serves 4-6

INGREDIENTS

1 tsp turmeric
1 tsp salt
1 kg/2 lb 4 oz cod fillet,
   skinned and cut into pieces
6 tbsp corn oil

4 green chillies
1 tsp fresh ginger root, finely
   chopped
1 tsp fresh garlic, crushed
2 medium onions, finely
   chopped

2 tomatoes, finely chopped
6 tbsp mustard oil
450 ml/³/4 pint/2 cups water
fresh coriander (cilantro)
   leaves, chopped, to garnish

1 Mix together the turmeric and salt in a small bowl.

2 Spoon the turmeric and salt mixture over the fish pieces.

3 Heat the oil in a frying-pan (skillet) and fry the fish pieces until pale yellow. Remove the fish with a perforated spoon and set aside.

4 Place the green chillies, ginger, garlic, onions, tomatoes and mustard oil in a pestle and mortar and grind to form a paste. Alternatively, work the ingredients in a food processor.

5 Transfer the spice paste to a saucepan and dry-fry until golden brown.

6 Remove the pan from the heat and gently place the fish pieces into the paste without breaking the fish up.

7 Return the pan to the heat, add the water and cook the fish, uncovered, over a medium heat for 15-20 minutes.

8 Garnish with chopped coriander (cilantro).

COOK'S TIP

In the hot and humid eastern plains that surround Bengal, the mustard plant flourishes, providing oil for cooking and spicy seeds for flavouring. Fish and seafood appear in many meals, often flavoured with mustard oil.

Prawns (Shrimp) with (Bell) Peppers

Serves 4

INGREDIENTS

450 g/1 lb frozen prawns
(shrimp)
1/2 bunch fresh coriander
(cilantro) leaves

1 tsp fresh garlic, crushed
1 tsp salt
1 medium green (bell) pepper,
sliced

1 medium red (bell) pepper
75 g/2³/4 oz/5¹/2 tbsp
unsalted butter

1 Defrost the prawns (shrimp). Once they are completely thawed, rinse them under cold running water twice. Drain the prawns (shrimp) thoroughly and place in a large mixing bowl.

2 Using a sharp knife, finely chop the bunch of fresh coriander (cilantro) leaves.

3 Add the garlic, salt and fresh, chopped coriander (cilantro) leaves to the prawns (shrimp), then set the bowl aside until required.

4 Deseed the (bell) peppers and cut into thin slices, using a sharp knife.

5 Melt the butter in a large frying pan (skillet). Add the prawns (shrimp) to the pan and stir-fry, stirring and tossing the prawns (shrimp) gently, for 10-12 minutes.

6 Add the (bell) peppers to the pan and fry for a further 3-5 minutes, stirring occasionally.

7 Transfer the prawns (shrimp) and (bell)

pepper to a serving dish and serve hot.

VARIATION

You could use large tiger prawns (shrimp) in this dish, if you prefer.

Prawns (Shrimp) with Spinach

Serves 4-6

INGREDIENTS

225 g/8 oz frozen prawns
  (shrimp)
350 g/12 oz canned spinach
  purée or frozen spinach,
  thawed and chopped

2 tomatoes
150 ml/¼ pint/⅔ cup oil
½ tsp mustard seeds
½ tsp onion seeds

1 tsp fresh ginger root, finely
  chopped
1 tsp fresh garlic, crushed
1 tsp chilli powder
1 tsp salt

1 Place the prawns
   (shrimp) in a bowl of
cold water and set aside to
defrost thoroughly.

2 Drain the can of
   spinach purée, if using.

3 Using a sharp knife,
   cut the tomatoes into
slices and set aside.

4 Heat the oil in a large
   frying pan (skillet).
Add the mustard and onion
seeds to the pan.

5 Reduce the heat and
   add the tomatoes,

spinach, ginger, garlic, chilli
powder and salt to the pan
and stir-fry for about
5-7 minutes.

6 Drain the prawns
   (shrimp) thoroughly.

7 Add the prawns
   (shrimp) to the spinach
mixture in the pan. Gently
stir the prawn (shrimp) and
spinach mixture until well
combined, cover and leave
to simmer over a low heat
for about 7-10 minutes.

8 Transfer the cooked
   prawns (shrimp) and

spinach to a serving dish
and serve hot.

COOK'S TIP

*If using frozen spinach, it
should be thawed and
squeezed dry before using.
You could use fresh spinach,
if you prefer.*

Tandoori-Style Prawns (Shrimp)

Serves 4

INGREDIENTS

10-12 king prawns (shrimp)
100 g/3^1/$_2$ oz/8 tbsp unsalted
    butter
1 tsp fresh ginger root, finely
    chopped
1 tsp fresh garlic, crushed
1 tsp chilli powder

^{1}/$_2$ tsp salt
1 tsp ground coriander
1 tsp ground cumin
fresh coriander (cilantro)
    leaves, finely chopped
a few drops of red food
    colouring

TO GARNISH:
8 lettuce leaves
1-2 green chillies, finely
    chopped
1 lemon, cut into wedges

1 Carefully remove the shells from the king prawns (shrimp).

2 Transfer the shelled prawns (shrimp) to a heatproof dish.

3 Melt the butter in a large saucepan.

4 Add the ginger, garlic, chilli powder, salt, ground coriander, ground cumin, fresh coriander (cilantro) leaves and the red food colouring to the butter and mix together until well combined.

5 Brush the melted butter and spice mixture over the prawns (shrimp).

6 Cook the prawns (shrimp) under a very hot pre-heated grill (broiler) for 10-12 minutes, turning once.

7 Serve the prawns (shrimp) on a bed of lettuce and garnish with finely chopped green chillies and lemon wedges.

COOK'S TIP

Though not essential, it is best to shell the prawns (shrimp) before cooking them as some people find it a bit awkward to shell them at the table.

Dried Prawns (Shrimp)

Serves 4

INGREDIENTS

200 g/7 oz dried prawns
(shrimp)
2 medium onions, sliced
3 green chillies, finely chopped
fresh coriander (cilantro)
leaves, finely chopped

300 ml/1/2 pint/1 1/4 cups oil
1 1/2 tsp fresh ginger root,
finely chopped
1 1/2 tsp fresh garlic, crushed
pinch of turmeric
1 tsp salt

1 tsp chilli powder, plus extra
to garnish
2 tbsp lemon juice

---

1 Soak the prawns
(shrimp) in a bowl of
cold water for about 2
hours. Drain the prawns
(shrimp) thoroughly and
rinse under cold running
water twice. Drain the
prawns (shrimp) again
thoroughly.

2 Heat 150 ml/1/4 pint/
2/3 cup of the oil in a
large saucepan. Add the
onions, 2 of the green
chillies and half of the
fresh coriander (cilantro)
to the pan and stir-fry until
the onions are golden.

3 Add the ginger, garlic,
turmeric, salt and chilli
powder to the pan and stir-
fry for a further 2 minutes
over a low heat. Set aside
until required.

4 Heat the remaining oil
in a separate saucepan.
Add the prawns (shrimp)
and fry, stirring
occasionally, until the
prawns (shrimp) are crisp.

5 Add the fried prawns
(shrimp) to the onions
and blend together. Return
the prawn (shrimp) and

onion mixture to the heat,
sprinkle with the lemon
juice and stir-fry for
3-5 minutes.

6 Transfer to a serving
dish, garnish with a
pinch of chilli powder and
serve with Chapatis (see
page 180).

VARIATION

*You could use 450 g/1 lb
fresh prawns (shrimp)
instead of the dried prawns
(shrimp), if you prefer.*

Prawns (Shrimp) with Tomatoes

Serves 4–6

INGREDIENTS

3 medium onions
1 green (bell) pepper
1 tsp fresh ginger root, finely
   chopped
1 tsp fresh garlic, crushed

1 tsp salt
1 tsp chilli powder
2 tbsp lemon juice
350 g/12 oz frozen prawns
   (shrimp)

3 tbsp oil
400 g/14 oz can tomatoes
fresh coriander (cilantro)
   leaves, to garnish

1 Using a sharp knife, slice the onions and the green (bell) pepper.

2 Place the ginger, garlic, salt and chilli powder in a small bowl and mix. Add the lemon juice and mix to form a paste.

3 Place the prawns (shrimp) in a bowl of cold water and set aside to defrost. Drain thoroughly.

4 Heat the oil in a medium-sized saucepan. Add the onions and fry until golden brown.

5 Add the spice paste to the onions, reduce the heat to low and cook, stirring and mixing well, for about 3 minutes.

6 Add the tomatoes, tomato juice and the green (bell) pepper, and cook for 5–7 minutes, stirring occasionally.

7 Add the defrosted prawns (shrimp) to the pan and cook the mixture for about 10 minutes, stirring occasionally. Garnish with fresh coriander (cilantro) leaves and serve hot with plain boiled rice and a crisp green salad.

COOK'S TIP

Fresh ginger root looks rather like a knobbly potato. The skin should be peeled, then the flesh either grated, finely chopped or sliced. Ginger is also available ground: this can be used as a substitute for fresh root ginger, but the fresh root is far superior.

Vegetables

A great many people in India are
vegetarians – possibly the majority. The reasons
for this are mainly religious, so over the years
Indians have used their imaginations to create a
vast majority of different vegetarian dishes. Spinach,
tomatoes, potatoes, green beans and cauliflower are
all commonly used in Indian cooking, but some
popular Indian vegetables, including aubergines
(eggplants), okra (lady's fingers) and mooli (white
radish), are less familiar in the West despite the fact
that they are now widely available.

In this chapter, I have included some simple but
delicious vegetarian dishes using these vegetables –
some in a sauce, some dry – that will help you
to familirize yourself with them.

In strict vegetarian households, neither fish
nor even eggs are even included in the diet, which
means it lacks protein (and certain vitamins). That
is why it is important to serve a dhaal (lentils) as
part of a vegetarian meal – all lentils are packed
with protein. A Raita (see page 216) makes an
excellent accompaniment to any vegetarian meal,
and for carbohydrate I think the best choice is plain
boiled rice or Pooris (see page 184).

Green Bean & Potato Curry

Serves 4

INGREDIENTS

300 ml/¹/₂ pint/1¹/₄ cups oil
1 tsp white cumin seeds
1 tsp mustard and onion seeds
4 dried red chillies
3 fresh tomatoes, sliced
1 tsp salt

1 tsp fresh ginger root, finely
  chopped
1 tsp fresh garlic, crushed
1 tsp chilli powder
200 g/7 oz green cut beans
2 medium potatoes, peeled
  and diced

300 ml/¹/₂ pint/1¹/₄ cups
  water
fresh coriander (cilantro)
  leaves, chopped
2 green chillies, finely chopped

1 Heat the oil in a large, heavy-based saucepan.

2 Add the white cumin seeds, mustard and onion seeds and dried red chillies to the saucepan, stirring well.

3 Add the tomato slices to the saucepan and stir-fry the mixture for 3-5 minutes.

4 Mix together the salt, ginger, garlic and chilli powder and spoon into the pan. Blend the whole mixture together.

5 Add the green beans and potatoes to the pan and stir-fry for about 5 minutes.

6 Add the water to the pan, reduce the heat and leave to simmer for 10-15 minutes, stirring occasionally.

7 Garnish the green bean and potato curry with chopped coriander (cilantro) leaves and green chillies and serve hot with cooked rice.

COOK'S TIP

Mustard seeds are often fried in oil or ghee to bring out their flavour before being combined with other ingredients.

Fried Cauliflower

Serves 4

INGREDIENTS

4 tbsp oil
$\frac{1}{2}$ tsp onion seeds
$\frac{1}{2}$ tsp mustard seeds
$\frac{1}{2}$ tsp fenugreek seeds

4 dried red chillies
1 small cauliflower, cut into
small florets
1 tsp salt

1 green (bell) pepper, diced

1 Heat the oil in a large, heavy-based saucepan.

2 Add the onion seeds, mustard seeds, fenugreek seeds and the dried red chillies to the pan, stirring to mix.

3 Reduce the heat and gradually add all of the cauliflower and the salt to the pan. Stir-fry the mixture for 7-10 minutes, coating the cauliflower florets thoroughly in the spice mixture.

4 Add the diced green (bell) pepper to the pan and stir-fry the mixture for 3-5 minutes.

5 Transfer the spicy fried cauliflower to a serving dish and serve hot.

COOK'S TIP

Onion seeds are small and black. They may be labelled as kalonj in Asian food stores. Onion seeds can be used instead of pepper, but have a spicier and more bitter taste.

VARIATION

For a weekend feast or a special occasion, this dish looks great made with baby cauliflowers instead of florets. Baby vegetables are more widely available nowadays, and the baby cauliflowers look very appealing on the plate. Peel off most of the outer leaves, leaving a few small leaves for decoration. Blanch the baby cauliflowers whole for 4 minutes and continue from step 3.

Aubergines (Eggplants) & Yogurt

Serves 4

INGREDIENTS
---

2 medium aubergines
  (eggplants)
4 tbsp oil
1 medium onion, sliced

1 tsp white cumin seeds
1 tsp chilli powder
1 tsp salt

3 tbsp natural yogurt
1/2 tsp mint sauce
chopped mint leaves, to
  garnish

---

1 Rinse the aubergines (eggplants) and pat dry with paper towels.

2 Place the aubergines (eggplants) in an ovenproof dish. Bake in a pre-heated oven, 160°C/425°F/Gas Mark 3, for 45 minutes. Remove the baked aubergines (eggplants) from the oven and leave to cool.

3 Slice each aubergine (eggplant) in half with a sharp knife and, using a spoon, scoop out the aubergine (eggplant) flesh and reserve.

4 Heat the oil in a heavy-based saucepan. Add the onions and cumin seeds and fry, stirring constantly, for 1-2 minutes.

5 Add the chilli powder, salt, natural yogurt and the mint sauce to the saucepan and stir the mixture well to combine.

6 Add the aubergine (eggplant) flesh to the onion and yogurt mixture in the pan and stir-fry for 5-7 minutes or until all of the liquid has been absorbed and the mixture is quite dry.

7 Transfer the aubergine (eggplant) and yogurt mixture to a serving dish and garnish with chopped mint leaves.

COOK'S TIP

Rich in protein and calcium, yogurt plays an important part in Indian cooking. Thick natural yogurt most closely resembles the yogurt made in many Indian homes.

Vegetable Kebabs (Kabobs)

Makes 10–12

INGREDIENTS

2 large potatoes, sliced
1 medium onion, sliced
$^1/_2$ medium cauliflower, cut into small florets
50 g/1$^3/_4$ oz peas
1 tbsp spinach purée (paste)
2–3 green chillies

fresh coriander (cilantro) leaves
1 tsp fresh ginger root, finely chopped
1 tsp fresh garlic, crushed
1 tsp ground coriander
1 pinch turmeric

1 tsp salt
50 g/1$^3/_4$ oz/1 cup breadcrumbs
300 ml/$^1/_2$ pint/1$^1/_4$ cups oil
fresh chilli strips, to garnish

1 Place the potatoes, onion and cauliflower florets in a pan of water and bring to the boil. Reduce the heat and leave to simmer until the potatoes are cooked through. Remove the vegetables from the pan with a perforated spoon and drain them thoroughly.

2 Add the peas and spinach to the vegetables and mix together, mashing down with a fork.

3 Using a sharp knife, finely chop the green chillies and fresh coriander (cilantro) leaves.

4 Mix the chillies and coriander (cilantro) with the ginger, garlic, ground coriander, turmeric and salt. Then blend the spice mixture into the vegetables, mixing with a fork to make a paste.

5 Scatter the breadcrumbs on to a large plate.

6 Break off 10–12 small balls from the spice paste. Flatten them with the palm of your hand to make flat, round shapes.

7 Dip each kebab (kabob) in the breadcrumbs, coating well.

8 Heat the oil in a heavy frying-pan (skillet) and fry the kebabs (kabobs) in batches until golden brown. Transfer to serving plates and garnish with fresh chilli strips.

Okra Curry

Serves 4

INGREDIENTS

450 g/1 lb okra (lady's fingers)
150 ml/¹/4 pint/²/3 cup oil
2 medium onions, sliced

3 green chillies, finely chopped
2 curry leaves
1 tsp salt

1 tomato, sliced
2 tbsp lemon juice
fresh coriander (cilantro)
    leaves

1 Rinse the okra (lady's fingers) and drain thoroughly. Using a sharp knife, chop and discard the ends of the okra (lady's fingers). Cut the okra (lady's fingers) into 2.5 cm/1 inch long pieces.

2 Heat the oil in a large, heavy frying-pan (skillet). Add the onions, green chillies, curry leaves and salt and mix together. Stir-fry the vegetables for 5 minutes.

3 Gradually add the okra (lady's fingers), mixing in gently with a perforated spoon. Stir-fry the vegetable mixture over a medium heat for 12-15 minutes.

4 Add the sliced tomato to the mixture and sprinkle over the lemon juice sparingly.

5 Garnish with coriander (cilantro) leaves, cover and leave to simmer for 3-5 minutes.

6 Transfer to serving plates and serve hot.

COOK'S TIP

Okra (lady's fingers) have a remarkable glutinous quality which naturally thickens curries and casseroles.

COOK'S TIP

When you buy fresh okra (lady's fingers), make sure they are not shrivelled and that they do not have any brown spots. Fresh okra (lady's fingers) will keep, tightly wrapped, for up to 3 days in the refrigerator.

Spinach & Cheese Curry

Serves 4

INGREDIENTS

300 ml/¹/₂ pint/1¹/₄ cups oil
200 g/7 oz panir, cubed (see
   Cook's Tip)

3 tomatoes, sliced
1 tsp ground cumin
1¹/₂ tsp ground chilli powder

1 tsp salt
400 g/14 oz spinach
3 green chillies

1 Heat the oil in a large frying pan (skillet). Add the cubed panir and fry, stirring occasionally, until golden brown.

2 Remove the panir from the frying pan (skillet) with a perforated spoon and leave to drain on kitchen paper.

3 Add the tomatoes to the remaining oil in the pan and stir-fry, breaking up the tomatoes, for 5 minutes.

4 Add the ground cumin, chilli powder and salt and mix well.

5 Add the spinach to the pan and stir-fry over a low heat for 7-10 minutes.

6 Add the green chillies and the panir and cook, stirring, for a further 2 minutes.

7 Transfer the curry to serving plates and serve hot with pooris or plain boiled rice.

VARIATION

You could used frozen spinach in this recipe. It should be thawed and squeezed dry before using.

COOK'S TIP

To make panir, boil 1 litre/ 1³/₄ pints/4¹/₂ cups milk slowly over a low heat, then add 2 tbsp lemon juice, stirring continuously and gently until the milk thickens and begins to curdle. Strain the curdled milk through a sieve. Set aside under a heavy weight for about 1¹/₂-2 hours to press to a flat shape about 1 cm/¹/₂ inch thick. Once set, the panir can be cut, like cheese, into whatever shape is required.

Vegetable Curry

Serves 4

INGREDIENTS

250 g/8 oz turnips or swede,
   peeled

1 aubergine (eggplant), leaf
   end trimmed

350 g/12 oz new potatoes,
   scrubbed

250 g/8 oz cauliflower

250 g/8 oz button mushrooms

1 large onion

250 g/8 oz carrots, peeled

6 tbsp vegetable ghee or oil

2 garlic cloves, crushed

5 cm/2 inch ginger root,
   chopped finely

1-2 fresh green chillies,
   seeded and chopped

1 tbsp paprika

2 tsp ground coriander

1 tbsp mild or medium curry
   powder or paste

450 ml/^{3}/4 pint/1^3/4 cups
   vegetable stock

400 g/14 oz can chopped
   tomatoes

1 green (bell) pepper, seeded
   and sliced

1 tbsp cornflour (cornstarch)

150 ml/^{1}/4 pint/^{2}/3 cup
   coconut milk

2-3 tbsp ground almonds

salt

fresh coriander (cilantro)
   sprigs, to garnish

1 Cut the turnips or swede, aubergine (eggplant) and potatoes into 1 cm/^{1}/2 inch cubes. Divide the cauliflower into small florets. Leave the mushrooms whole and slice the onion and carrots.

2 Heat the ghee or oil in a large saucepan, add the onion, turnip, potato and cauliflower and cook gently for 3 minutes, stirring frequently. Add the garlic, ginger, chillies, paprika, ground coriander and curry powder or paste and cook for 1 minute.

3 Add the stock, tomatoes, aubergine (eggplant) and mushrooms and season with salt. Cover and simmer for 30 minutes or until tender. Add the (bell) pepper and carrots, cover and cook for a further 5 minutes.

4 Blend the cornflour (cornstarch) with the coconut milk and stir into the mixture. Add ground almonds and simmer for 2 minutes, stirring all the time. Transfer to serving plates and garnish with fresh coriander (cilantro).

Stuffed Rice Pancakes

Makes 6–8

INGREDIENTS

200 g/7 oz rice and 50 g/1³/₄
oz *urid dhaal*, or 200 g/7
oz ground rice and 50
g/1³/₄ oz) *urid dhaal* flour
(*ata*)
425–600 ml/³/₄–1 pint water
1 tsp salt

4 tbsp oil

FILLING:
4 medium potatoes, diced
3 green chillies, chopped
¹/₂ tsp turmeric
1 tsp salt

150 ml/¹/₄ pint/²/₃ cup oil
1 tsp mustard and onion seeds
3 dried chillies
4 curry leaves
2 tbsp lemon juice

1 To make the *dosas* (pancakes), soak the rice and *urid dhaal* for 3 hours. Grind the rice and *urid dhaal* to a smooth consistency, adding water if necessary. Set aside for a further 3 hours to ferment. Alternatively, if you are using ground rice and *urid dhaal* flour (*ata*), mix together in a bowl. Add the water and salt and stir until a batter is formed.

2 Heat about 1 tbsp of oil in a non-stick frying-pan (skillet). Using a ladle, spoon the batter into the pan then tilt the pan to spread the mixture over the base. Cover and cook over a medium heat for 2 minutes. Remove the lid and turn the *dosa* over very carefully. Pour a little oil around the edge, cover and cook for a further 2 minutes. Repeat with the remaining batter.

3 To make the filling, boil the potatoes in a pan of water. Add the chillies, turmeric and salt and cook until the potatoes are soft enough to be lightly mashed.

4 Heat the oil in a saucepan and fry the mustard and onion seeds, dried red chillies and curry leaves for about 1 minute. Pour the spice mixture over the mashed potatoes, then sprinkle over the lemon juice and mix well. Spoon the potato filling on one half of the *dosas* (pancakes) and fold the other half over the filling.

Potatoes with Spices & Onions

Serves 4

INGREDIENTS

6 tbsp oil
2 medium-sized onions,
    chopped finely
1 tsp fresh ginger root, finely
    chopped
1 tsp fresh garlic, crushed
1 tsp chilli powder
1 1/2 tsp ground cumin

1 1/2 tsp ground coriander
1 tsp salt
400 g/14 oz can new potatoes
1 tbsp lemon juice
1 green chilli, finely chopped,
    to garnish

BAGHAAR:
3 tbsp oil
3 dried red chillies
1/2 tsp onion seeds
1/2 tsp mustard seeds
1/2 tsp fenugreek seeds

1 Heat the oil in a large saucepan. Add the onions and fry, stirring, until golden brown. Reduce the heat, add the ginger, garlic, chilli powder, ground cumin, ground coriander and salt and stir-fry for about 1 minute. Remove the pan from the heat and set aside until required.

2 Drain the water from the potatoes. Add the potatoes to the onion and spice mixture. Sprinkle over the lemon juice and mix well.

3 To make the *baghaar*, heat some more oil in a separate saucepan. Add the chopped red chillies, onion seeds, mustard seeds and fenugreek seeds and fry, stirring constantly, until the seeds turn a shade darker. Remove the pan from the heat and pour the *baghaar* over the spicy potato mixture.

4 Garnish with finely chopped chilli and serve immediately.

COOK'S TIP

You could also serve these spicy potatoes and onions, for a change, with roast lamb or lamb chops.

Mooli (White Radish) Curry

Serves 4

INGREDIENTS

450 g/1 lb mooli (white
radish), preferably with
leaves
1 tbsp *moong dhaal*

600 ml/1 pint/2^1/$_2$ cups water
1 medium onion
150 ml/^{1}/$_4$ pint/^{2}/$_3$ cup oil

1 tsp fresh garlic, crushed
1 tsp red chillies, crushed
1 tsp salt

1 Rinse, peel and roughly slice the mooli (white radish) together with its leaves.

2 Place the mooli (white radish), the leaves (if using) and the *moong dhaal* in a large saucepan and pour over the water. Bring to the boil and simmer until the mooli (white radish) is soft enough to be handled.

3 Drain the mouli (white radish) thoroughly and squeeze out any excess water, using your hands.

4 Using a sharp knife, slice the onion thinly.

5 Heat the oil in a saucepan. Add the sliced onion, crushed garlic, crushed red chillies and salt and fry, stirring occasionally, until the onions have softened and turned a light golden brown colour.

6 Stir the mooli (white radish) mixture into the spiced onion mixture and combine well. Reduce the heat and continue cooking, stirring frequently, for about 3-5 minutes.

7 Transfer the mooli (white radish) curry to individual serving plates and serve hot with Chapatis (see page 180).

COOK'S TIP

The vegetable used in this recipe, mooli (white parsnip), looks a bit like a parsnip without the tapering end and is now sold in most supermarkets as well as in Indian and Pakistani grocers.

Aubergines (Eggplants) in Pickling Spices

Serves 4

INGREDIENTS

2 tsp ground coriander
2 tsp ground cumin
2 tsp desiccated coconut
2 tsp sesame seeds
1 tsp mixed mustard and
    onion seeds
300 ml/¹/₂ pint/1¹/₄ cups oil
3 medium onions, sliced
1 tsp fresh ginger root, finely
    chopped

1 tsp fresh garlic, crushed
¹/₂ tsp turmeric
1¹/₂ tsp chilli powder
1¹/₂ tsp salt
3 medium aubergines
    (eggplants), halved
    lengthwise
1 tbsp tamarind paste
300 ml/¹/₂ pint/1¹/₄ cups
    water

BAGHAAR:
1 tsp mixed onion and
    mustard seeds
1 tsp cumin seeds
4 dried red chillies
150 ml/¹/₄ pint/²/₃ cup oil
coriander (cilantro) leaves
1 green chilli, finely chopped
3 hard-boiled (hard-cooked)
    eggs, halved, to garnish

1 Dry-roast the coriander, cumin, coconut, sesame seeds and mustard and onion seeds in a pan. Grind and set aside.

2 Fry the onions in oil in a frying pan (skillet). Reduce the heat and add salt, ginger, garlic, turmeric and chilli powder. When cool, grind into a paste.

3 Make 4 cuts or slits across each aubergine (eggplant) half. Blend the spices with the onion paste and spoon into the slits.

4 Mix the tamarind paste and 3 tbsp water to make a fine paste.

5 For the *baghaar*, fry the onion and mustard seeds, cumin seeds and chillies in the oil. Reduce the heat and place the aubergines (eggplants) into the heated *baghaar*. Stir in the tamarind paste and the rest of the water and cook for 15-20 minutes. Add the coriander (cilantro) and green chillies. When cool, transfer to a serving dish and garnish with the eggs.

Dumplings in Yogurt Sauce

Serves 4

INGREDIENTS

DUMPLINGS:
100 g/3^1/$_2$ oz/^{3}/$_4$ cup gram flour
1 tsp chilli powder
^{1}/$_2$ tsp salt
^{1}/$_2$ tsp bicarbonate of soda (baking soda)
1 medium onion, finely chopped
2 green chillies
fresh coriander (cilantro)

150 ml/^{1}/$_4$ pint/^{2}/$_3$ cup water
300 ml/^{1}/$_2$ pint/1^1/$_4$ cups oil

YOGURT SAUCE:
300 ml/^{1}/$_2$ pint/1^1/$_4$ cups yogurt
3 tbsp gram flour
150 ml/^{1}/$_4$ pint/^{2}/$_3$ cup water
1 tsp fresh ginger root, chopped
1 tsp fresh garlic, crushed

1^1/$_2$ tsp chilli powder
1^1/$_2$ tsp salt
^{1}/$_2$ tsp turmeric
1 tsp ground coriander
5 ml/1 tsp ground cumin

SEASONED DRESSING:
150 ml/^{1}/$_4$ pint/^{2}/$_3$ cup oil
1 tsp white cumin seeds
6 red dried chillies

1 To make the dumplings, sieve the gram flour into a large bowl. Add the chilli powder, salt, soda, onion, green chillies and coriander (cilantro) and mix. Add the water and mix to form a thick paste. Heat the oil in a frying-pan (skillet). Drop teaspoonfuls of the paste in the oil and fry over a medium heat, until golden.

2 To make the sauce, place the yogurt in a bowl and whisk with the gram flour and the water. Add all of the spices and garlic, and mix well. Push this mixture through a large sieve into a saucepan. Bring the sauce to a boil over a low heat while stirring continuously. If the yogurt sauce becomes too thick add a little extra water.

3 Pour the sauce into a deep serving dish and arrange the dumplings on top. Keep warm.

4 To make the dressing, heat the oil in a frying-pan (skillet). Add the white cumin seeds and the dried red chillies and fry until darker in colour. Pour the dressing over the dumplings and serve hot.

Potato Curry

Serves 4

INGREDIENTS
---

3 medium potatoes	4 curry leaves	1 pinch turmeric
150 ml/^{1}/4 pint/^{2}/3 cup oil	1 tsp ground cumin	1 tsp salt
1 tsp onion seeds	1 tsp ground coriander	1^1/2 tsp *aamchoor* (dried
^{1}/2 tsp fennel seeds	1 tsp chilli powder	mango powder)

1 Peel and rinse the potatoes. Using a sharp knife, cut each potato into six slices.

2 Boil the potato slices in a saucepan of water for about 12-15 minutes, until they are just cooked, but not mushy (test by piercing with a sharp knife or a skewer). Drain and set aside until required.

3 In a separate saucepan heat the oil. Reduce the heat and add the onion seeds, the fennel seeds and the curry leaves, stirring them continuously

4 Remove the pan from the heat and add the ground cumin, coriander, chilli powder, turmeric, salt and the *aamchoor* (dried mango powder), stirring well to combine.

5 Return the pan to the heat and stir-fry the spicy mixture for about 1 minute.

6 Pour this mixture over the cooked potatoes, mix together well without breaking up the potatoes too much, and stir-fry over a low heat for about 5 minutes.

7 Transfer the potato curry to serving dishes and serve immediately.

COOK'S TIP

Traditionally, Semolina Dessert (see page 244) is served to follow Potato Curry.

Courgettes (Zucchini) & Fenugreek Seeds

Serves 4

INGREDIENTS

6 tbsp oil	chopped finely	2 tomatoes, sliced
1 medium onion, finely	1 tsp fresh garlic, crushed	fresh coriander (cilantro)
chopped	1 tsp chilli powder	leaves, plus extra to
3 green chillies, finely chopped	450 g/1 lb courgettes	garnish
1 tsp fresh ginger root,	(zucchini) sliced	2 tsp fenugreek seeds

1 Heat the oil in a large frying pan (skillet).

2 Add the onion, green chillies, ginger, garlic and chilli powder to the pan, stirring well to combine.

3 Add the sliced courgettes (zucchini) and the sliced tomatoes to the pan and stir-fry for 5-7 minutes.

4 Add the cilantro (coriander) and fenugreek seeds to the courgette (zucchini) mixture in the pan and stir-fry for 5 minutes.

5 Remove the pan from the heat and transfer the courgette (zucchini) and fenugreek seed mixture to serving dishes. Garnish and serve hot with Chapatis (see page 180).

COOK'S TIP

Both the leaves and seeds of fenugreek are used, but the stalks and root should be discarded, as they have a bitter taste. Fresh fenugreek is sold in bunches. Fenugreek seeds are flat and yellowish brown in colour. You could use coriander seeds instead of the fenugreek seeds, if you prefer.

Green Pumpkin Curry

Serves 4

INGREDIENTS

150 ml/¹/₄ pint/²/₃ cup oil
2 medium-sized onions, sliced
¹/₂ tsp white cumin seeds
450 g/1 lb green pumpkin,
    cubed

1 tsp *aamchoor* (dried mango
    powder)
1 tsp fresh ginger root, finely
    chopped

1 tsp fresh garlic, crushed
1 tsp crushed red chilli
¹/₂ tsp salt
300 ml/¹/₂ pint/1¹/₄ cups
    water

1 Heat the oil in a large frying pan (skillet). Add the onions and cumin seeds and fry, stirring occasionally, until a light golden brown colour.

2 Add the cubed pumpkin to the pan and stir-fry for 3-5 minutes over a low heat.

3 Mix the *aamchoor* (dried mango powder), ginger, garlic, chilli and salt

4 Add the spice mixture to the onion mixture, stirring well to combine.

5 Add the water, cover and cook over a low heat for 10-15 minutes, stirring occasionally.

6 Transfer to serving plates and serve with Gram Flour Bread (see page 176).

VARIATION

You can use ordinary pumpkin for this recipe, if you prefer.

COOK'S TIP

Cumin seeds are popular with Indian cooks because of their warm, pungent flavour and aroma. The seeds are sold whole or ground, and are usually included as one of the flavourings in garam masala.

Potatoes & Peas

Serves 2-4

INGREDIENTS

150 ml/¹/4 pint/²/3 cup oil
3 medium onions, sliced
1 tsp fresh garlic, crushed
1 tsp fresh ginger root, finely
  chopped
1 tsp chilli powder

¹/2 tsp turmeric
1 tsp salt
2 fresh green chillies, finely
  chopped
300 ml/¹/2 pint/1¹/4 cups
  water

3 medium potatoes
100 g/3¹/2 oz peas
finely chopped red chillies, to
  garnish

1 Heat the oil in a large frying-pan (skillet). Add the onions to the pan and fry them, stirring occasionally, until they are golden brown.

2 Mix together the garlic, ginger, chilli powder, turmeric, salt and fresh green chillies. Add the spice mixture to the onions in the pan.

3 Stir in 150 ml/¹/4 pint/²/3 cup of the water, cover and cook until the onions are cooked through.

4 Meanwhile, peel and rinse the potatoes then cut them into six slices each, using a sharp knife.

5 Add the potato slices to the mixture in the pan and stir-fry for 5 minutes.

6 Add the peas and the remaining 150 ml/¹/4 pint/²/3 cup of the water to the pan, cover and cook for 7-10 minutes.

7 Transfer the potatoes and peas to serving plates and serve garnished with finely chopped red chillies.

COOK'S TIP

Turmeric is an aromatic root which is dried and ground to produce the distinctive bright yellow-orange powder used in many Indian dishes. It has a warm, aromatic smell and a full, somewhat musty taste.

Chick-pea (Garbanzo Bean) Curry

Serves 4

INGREDIENTS

6 tbsp oil
2 medium onions, sliced
1 tsp fresh ginger root, finely
  chopped
1 tsp ground cumin

1 tsp ground coriander
1 tsp fresh garlic, crushed
1 tsp chilli powder
2 fresh green chillies
fresh coriander (cilantro)
  leaves

150 ml/^{1}/4 pint/^{2}/3 cup water
1 large potato
400 g/14 oz can chick-peas
  (garbanzo beans), drained
1 tbsp lemon juice

1 Heat the oil in a large saucepan.

2 Add the sliced onions to the pan and fry, stirring occasionally, until golden brown.

3 Reduce the heat, then add the ginger, ground cumin, ground coriander, garlic, chilli powder, chopped fresh green chillies and fresh coriander (cilantro) leaves to the saucepan, stirring the ingredients constantly for about 2 minutes.

4 Add the water to the mixture in the pan and stir to mix.

5 Using a sharp knife, cut the potato into small dice.

6 Add the potatoes and the drained chick peas (garbanzo beans) to the mixture in the pan, cover and leave to simmer, stirring occasionally, for 5-7 minutes.

7 Sprinkle the lemon juice over the curry.

8 Transfer the chick pea (garbanzo bean) curry to serving dishes. Serve the curry hot with chapati, if you wish.

COOK'S TIP

Using canned chick-peas (garbanzo beans) saves time, but you can use dried chick-peas (garbanzo beans) if you prefer. Soak them overnight, then boil them for 15-20 minutes or until soft.

Egg Curry

Serves 4

INGREDIENTS

4 tbsp oil
1 medium onion, sliced
1 fresh red chilli, finely
    chopped
1/2 tsp chilli powder

1/2 tsp fresh ginger root, finely
    chopped
1/2 tsp fresh garlic, crushed
4 medium eggs

1 firm tomato, sliced
fresh coriander (cilantro)
    leaves

1 Heat the oil in a large saucepan.

2 Add the sliced onion to the pan and fry until just softened and a light golden colour.

3 Add the red chilli, chilli powder, ginger and garlic and stir-fry the mixture, over a low heat, for about 1 minute.

4 Add the eggs and tomatoes to the mixture in the pan and continue cooking, stirring gently to break up the eggs when they begin to cook, for 3-5 minutes.

5 Sprinkle the fresh coriander (cilantro) leaves over the mixture.

6 Transfer the egg curry to serving plates and serve hot with Paratas (see page 174), if you wish.

COOK'S TIP

Both the leaves and finely chopped stems of coriander (cilantro) are used in Indian cooking, to flavour dishes and as edible garnishes. It has a very distinctive and pronounced taste.

COOK'S TIP

Eggs contain high quality protein, fat, iron and vitamins A, B and D, although they are also high in cholesterol.

Mixed Vegetables

Serves 4

INGREDIENTS

300 ml/^{1}/2 pint/1^1/4 cups oil
1 tsp mustard seeds
1 tsp onion seeds
^{1}/2 tsp white cumin seeds
3-4 curry leaves, chopped
450 g/1 lb onions, finely
  chopped
3 medium tomatoes, chopped
^{1}/2 red, ^{1}/2 green (bell) pepper,
  sliced

1 tsp fresh ginger root, finely
  chopped
1 tsp fresh garlic, crushed
1 tsp chilli powder
^{1}/4 tsp turmeric
1 tsp salt
425 ml/^{3}/4 pint/2 cups water
2 medium potatoes, peeled
  and cut into pieces

^{1}/2 cauliflower, cut into small
  florets
4 medium carrots, peeled and
  sliced
3 green chillies, finely chopped
fresh coriander (cilantro)
  leaves
1 tbsp lemon juice

1 Heat the oil in a large saucepan. Add the mustard, onion and white cumin seeds along with the curry leaves and fry until they turn a shade darker.

2 Add the onions to the pan and fry over a medium heat until golden.

3 Add the tomatoes and (bell) peppers and stir-fry for about 5 minutes.

4 Add the ginger, garlic, chilli powder, turmeric and salt and mix well.

5 Add 300 ml/^{1}/2 pint/ 1^1/4 cups of the water, cover and leave to simmer for 10-12 minutes.

6 Add the potatoes, cauliflower, carrots, green chillies and coriander (cilantro) leaves and stir-fry for about 5 minutes.

7 Add the remaining 150 ml/^{1}/4 pint/^{2}/3 cup of water and the lemon juice, stirring to combine. Cover and leave to simmer for about 15 minutes, stirring occasionally.

8 Transfer the mixed vegetables to serving plates and serve at once.

Potato & Cauliflower Curry

Serves 4

INGREDIENTS

150 ml/^{1}/4 pint/^{2}/3 cup oil
^{1}/2 tsp white cumin seeds
4 dried red chillies
2 medium onions, sliced
1 tsp fresh ginger root, finely
   chopped

1 tsp fresh garlic, crushed
1 tsp chilli powder
1 tsp salt
1 pinch of turmeric
3 medium potatoes, peeled
   and sliced

^{1}/2 cauliflower, cut into small
   florets
2 green chillies (optional)
fresh coriander (cilantro)
   leaves
150 ml/^{1}/4 pint/^{2}/3 cup water

1 Heat the oil in a large saucepan.

2 Add the white cumin seeds and dried red chillies to the pan, stirring to mix.

3 Add the sliced onions to the pan and fry, stirring occasionally, until golden brown.

4 Mix the ginger, garlic, chilli powder, salt and turmeric together in a separate bowl, then add the spice mixture to the onions and stir-fry for about 2 minutes.

5 Add the peeled and sliced potatoes and the cauliflower florets to the onion and spice mixture, stirring thoroughly to coat all the vegetables in the spice mixture.

6 Reduce the heat and add the green chillies (if using), fresh coriander (cilantro) leaves and water to the pan. Cover and leave the mixture to simmer for about 10-15 minutes.

7 Transfer the potato and cauliflower curry to warm serving plates and serve immediately.

COOK'S TIP

Always handle chillies with caution, preferably wearing rubber gloves because the juices are extremely pungent. Wash your hands thoroughly after preparing and handling chillies and do not allow your fingers near your eyes as this can be very painful.

Dry Split Okra

Serves 4

INGREDIENTS

450 g/1 lb okra
150 ml/¼ pint/⅔ cup oil
100 g/3½ oz/½ cup dried
  onions

2 tsp *aamchoor* (dried mango
  powder)
1 tsp ground cumin

1 tsp chilli powder
1 tsp salt

1 Prepare the okra by cutting the ends off and discarding them. Using a sharp knife, carefully split the okra down the middle without cutting through them completely.

2 Heat the oil in a large saucepan. Add the dried onions and fry until they are crisp.

3 Remove the fried onions from the pan with a perforated spoon and leave them to drain thoroughly on sheets of paper towel.

4 When cool enough to handle, roughly tear the dried onions and place in a large bowl.

5 Add the *aamchoor* (dried mango), ground cumin, chilli powder and salt to the dried onions and blend well together.

6 Spoon the onion and spice mixture into the split okra.

7 Re-heat the oil in the saucepan.

8 Gently add the okra to the hot oil and cook over a low heat for about 10–12 minutes.

9 Transfer the cooked okra to a serving dish and serve immediately.

COOK'S TIP

Ground cumin has a warm, pungent aromatic flavour and is used extensively in Indian cooking. It is a good storecupboard standby.

Tomato Curry

Serves 4

INGREDIENTS

400 g/14 oz can tomatoes
1 tsp fresh ginger root,
    chopped finely
1 tsp fresh garlic, crushed
1 tsp chilli powder
1 tsp salt
1/2 tsp ground coriander

1/2 tsp ground cumin
4 tbsp oil
1/2 tsp onion seeds
1/2 tsp mustard seeds
1/2 tsp fenugreek seeds
1 pinch white cumin seeds
3 dried red chillies

2 tbsp lemon juice
3 eggs, hard-boiled (hard-
    cooked)
fresh coriander (cilantro)
    leaves

1 Place the tomatoes in a large mixing bowl.

2 Add the ginger, garlic, chilli powder, salt, ground coriander and ground cumin to the tomatoes and blend well.

3 Heat the oil in a saucepan. Add the onion, mustard, fenugreek and white cumin seeds, and the dried red chillies, and stir-fry for about 1 minute. Remove the pan from the heat.

4 Add the tomato mixture to the spicy oil mixture and return to the heat. Stir-fry the mixture for about 3 minutes, then reduce the heat and cook with the lid ajar for 7-10 minutes, stirring occasionally.

5 Sprinkle over the lemon juice sparingly.

6 Transfer the tomato curry to a serving dish, set aside and keep warm until required.

7 Shell and halve the hard-boiled (hard-cooked) eggs, then gently add them, yolk end down, to the tomato curry.

8 Garnish with fresh coriander (cilantro) leaves and serve hot.

COOK'S TIP

This tomato curry can be made in advance and frozen, as it freezes particularly well.

Breads & Grains

The most common Indian breads are chapati, paratas and poori, all of which can be made with wholemeal flour – so they are very healthy foods. Indian breads are made as individual portions, and I suggest you allow 2 per person.

Rice is served with almost every meal in India, so the Indians have created a variety of ways of cooking it. Whatever the dish, the aim is to produce dry, separate grained rice that is cooked yet still has some 'bite' to it. Basmati rice is the type I recommend, because it cooks very well and gives an excellent result. It is best to soak it for about 20-30 minutes before cooking, to prevent the grains from sticking to each other. As a rough guide, allow about 75 g/2³/₄ oz rice per person.

There are at least 30 different types of lentil to be found in India, but the 4 most commonly used are moong, masoor, chana and urid. Rich in protein, lentils make ideal accompaniments to vegetable curries. Lentils are also delicious cooked with a variety of meats. Before cooking, wash the lentils at least twice and if you have time, soak them for 3 hours – this will also cut down on the cooking time.

Lemon Dhaal

Serves 4

INGREDIENTS

100 g/3^1/2 oz/^{1}/2 cup
   masoor dhaal
1 tsp fresh ginger root, finely
   chopped
1 tsp fresh garlic, crushed
1 tsp chilli powder
^{1}/2 tsp turmeric

425 ml/^{3}/4 pint/2 cups water
1 tsp salt
3 tbsp lemon juice
2 green chillies
fresh coriander (cilantro)
   leaves

BAGHAAR:
150 ml/^{1}/4 pint/^{2}/3 cup oil
4 whole garlic cloves
6 dried red chillies
1 tsp white cumin seeds

1 Rinse the *masoor dhaal* and place in a large saucepan.

2 Add the ginger, garlic, chilli powder and turmeric to the *dhaal*. Stir in 300 ml/^{1}/2 pint/1^1/4 cups of the water and bring to a boil over a medium heat with the lid left slightly ajar until the *dhaal* is soft enough to be mashed.

3 Mash the *dhaal*. Add the salt, lemon juice and 150 ml/^{1}/4 pint/^{2}/3 cup

of the water, stir and mix well. It should be of a fairly smooth consistency.

4 Add the green chillies and fresh coriander (cilantro) leaves to the *dhaal* and set aside.

5 To make the *baghaar*, heat the oil in a pan. Add the garlic, red chillies and white cumin seeds and fry for about 1 minute. Turn off the heat, then when the heat has been reduced pour the *baghaar*

over the *dhaal*. If the *dhaal* is too runny cook over a medium heat with the lid off for 3-5 minutes.

6 Transfer to a serving dish and serve hot.

COOK'S TIP

This dish is a good accompaniment to Beef Khorma with Almonds (see page 50).

White Lentils

Serves 2-4

INGREDIENTS

100 g/3¹/₂ oz/¹/₂ cup *urid dhaal*
1 tsp fresh ginger root, finely chopped
600 ml/1 pint/2¹/₂ cups water

1 tsp salt
1 tsp pepper
2 tbsp pure or vegetable ghee
2 cloves garlic, peeled

2 red chillies, finely chopped
fresh mint leaves, to garnish

1 Rinse the lentils twice, removing any stones.

2 Place the lentils and ginger in a large saucepan.

3 Add the water and bring to a boil, covered, over a medium heat for about 30 minutes. Check to see whether the lentils are cooked by rubbing them between your finger and thumb. If they are still a little hard in the middle, cook for a further 5-7 minutes. If necessary, remove the lid and cook until any remaining water has evaporated.

4 Add the salt and coarsely ground black pepper to the lentils, mix well and set aside.

5 Heat the ghee in a separate saucepan. Add the cloves of garlic and chopped red chillies, and stir well to mix.

6 Pour the garlic and chilli mixture over the lentils and then garnish with the fresh mint leaves.

7 Transfer the white lentils to serving dishes and serve hot with Chapatis (see page 180).

COOK'S TIP

Urid dhaal *are small, round white split lentils, which are popular with northern Indians. Dhaals are usually labelled simply 'lentils' in most supermarkets.*

Onion Dhaal

Serves 4

INGREDIENTS

100 g/3^{1}/2 oz/^{1}/2 cup *masoor dhaal*
6 tbsp oil
1 small bunch spring onions (scallions), trimmed and chopped, including the green part

1 tsp fresh ginger root, finely chopped
1 tsp fresh garlic, crushed
^{1}/2 tsp chilli powder
^{1}/2 tsp turmeric
300 ml/^{1}/2 pint/1^{1}/4 cups water

1 tsp salt
1 fresh green chilli, finely chopped
fresh coriander (cilantro) leaves

1 Rinse the *masoor dhaal* lentils and set aside until required.

2 Heat the oil in a saucepan. Add the chopped spring onions (scallions) to the pan and fry, stirring constantly, until lightly browned.

3 Reduce the heat and add the ginger, garlic, chilli powder and turmeric to the pan. Stir-fry the spring onions (scallions) with the spices.

4 Add the lentils and mix to blend together.

5 Add the water to the lentil mixture in the pan, reduce the heat further and cook for 20-25 minutes.

6 When the lentils are cooked thoroughly, add the salt and stir with a wooden spoon to gently combine.

7 Garnish the onion lentils with the

chopped green chillies and fresh coriander (cilantro) leaves. Transfer the onion lentils to a serving dish and serve immediately.

COOK'S TIP

Masoor dhaal are small, round, pale orange split lentils. They turn a pale yellow colour when cooked.

Oil-Dressed Dhaal

Serves 4

INGREDIENTS

75 g/2³/₄ oz/5 tbsp *masoor dhaal*
50 g/1³/₄ oz/4 tbsp *moong dhaal*
450 ml/³/₄ pint/2 cups water

1 tsp fresh ginger root, finely chopped
1 tsp fresh garlic, crushed
2 red chillies, chopped
1 tsp salt

TARKA (BAGHAAR):
2 tbsp ghee
1 medium onion, sliced
mixed mustard and onion seeds

1 Rinse the lentils, removing any stones.

2 Place the lentils in a large saucepan and gradually pour over the water, stirring. Add the ginger, garlic and chopped red chillies and bring to a boil over a medium heat, half covered with a lid, until the lentils are soft enough to be mashed (about 15-20 minutes).

3 Mash the lentils, adding a little more water if necessary to form a thick sauce.

4 Add the salt to the lentil mixture and stir to combine. Transfer the lentils to a heatproof serving dish.

5 Just before serving, melt the ghee in a small saucepan. Add the sliced onion and fry until golden brown. Add the mustard and onion seeds and stir to mix.

6 Pour the onion mixture over the lentils while still hot. Transfer to a serving dish and serve immediately.

COOK'S TIP

This dish makes a a very good accompaniment, especially for a dry vegetarian or meat curry. It also freezes well – simply re-heat it in a saucepan or covered in the oven.

Black-Eye Beans (Peas)

Serves 4

INGREDIENTS
---

150 g/5^1/2 oz/1 cup black-eye
  beans (peas)
300 ml/^{1}/2 pint/1^1/4 cups oil
2 medium onions, sliced
1 tsp fresh ginger root, finely
  chopped

1 tsp fresh garlic, crushed
1 tsp chilli powder
1^1/2 tsp salt
1^1/2 tsp ground coriander
1^1/2 tsp ground cumin
150 ml/^{1}/4 pint/^{2}/3 cup water

2 red chillies, finely sliced
fresh coriander (cilantro)
  leaves
1 tbsp lemon juice

1 Rinse and soak the black-eye beans (peas) in a bowl of water overnight.

2 Place the black-eye beans (peas) in a pan of water and bring to a boil over a low heat for about 30 minutes. Drain the beans (peas) thoroughly and set aside.

3 Heat the oil in a pan. Add the onions and fry until golden brown. Add the ginger, garlic, chilli powder, salt, ground

coriander and ground cumin and stir-fry the mixture for 3-5 minutes.

4 Add the water to the pan, cover and cook the mixture until all of the water has completely evaporated.

5 Add the boiled black-eye beans (peas), red chilli slices and coriander (cilantro) leaves to the onions and stir to blend together. Stir-fry the bean (pea) mixture for 3-5 minutes.

6 Transfer the black-eye beans (peas) to a serving dish and sprinkle over the lemon juice. Serve hot or cold.

COOK'S TIP

Black-eye beans (peas) are oval-shaped, grey or beige beans (peas) with a dark dot in the centre. They have a slightly smoky flavour. They are sold canned as well as dried.

Dry Moong Dhaal

Serves 4

INGREDIENTS

150 g/5^1/2 oz/1 cup *moong dhaal*
1 tsp fresh ginger root, finely chopped
^{1}/2 tsp ground cumin
^{1}/2 tsp ground coriander

1 tsp fresh garlic, crushed
^{1}/2 tsp chilli powder
600 ml/1 pint/2^1/2 cups water
1 tsp salt

BAGHAAR:
100 g/3^1/2 oz/8 tbsp unsalted butter
5 dried red chillies
1 tsp white cumin seeds

1 Rinse the lentils, removing any stones.

2 Place the lentils in a pan. Add the ginger, ground cumin, ground coriander, garlic and chilli powder, and stir to mix.

3 Pour in the water to cover the lentil mixture. Cook over a medium heat, stirring, until the lentils are soft but not mushy.

4 Add the salt to the lentils and stir to mix.

Transfer to a serving dish and keep warm.

5 Meanwhile, make the *baghaar*. Melt the butter in a saucepan. Add the dried red chillies and white cumin seeds and fry until they begin to pop.

6 Pour the *baghaar* over the lentils and serve hot with chapati and a vegetable or meat curry.

COOK'S TIP

Dried red chillies are the quickest way to add heat to a dish.

COOK'S TIP

Moong dhaal *are tear-drop-shaped yellow split lentils, more popular in northern India than in the south.*

Spinach & Chana Dhaal

Serves 4-6

INGREDIENTS

4 tbsp *chana dhaal*
6 tbsp oil
1 tsp mixed onion and
    mustard seeds
4 dried red chillies

400-450 g/14-16 oz can
    spinach, drained
1 tsp fresh ginger root,
    chopped finely
1 tsp ground coriander

1 tsp ground cumin
1 tsp salt
1 tsp chilli powder
2 tbsp lemon juice
1 green chilli, to garnish

1 Soak the *chana dhaal* in a bowl of warm water for at least 3 hours, preferably overnight.

2 Drain the lentils then place them in a saucepan, cover with water, bring to the boil and cook for 30 minutes.

3 Heat the oil in another smaller saucepan. Add the mixed onion and mustard seeds and the dried red chillies and fry them, stirring constantly, until the mixed seeds turn a shade darker.

4 Add the drained spinach to the pan, mixing gently.

5 Add the ginger, ground coriander, ground cumin, salt and chilli powder to the mixture in the pan. Reduce the heat and gently stir-fry the mixture for about 7-10 minutes.

6 Add the lentils to the saucepan and blend into the spicy spinach mixture well to combine, stirring gently so that it does not break up.

7 Transfer the mixture to a serving dish. Sprinkle over the lemon juice and garnish with the green chilli. Serve immediately.

COOK'S TIP

Very similar in appearance to moong dhaal – *the yellow split peas* – chana dhaal *has slightly less shiny grains. It is used as a binding agent and may be bought from Indian and Pakistani grocers.*

Strained Dhaal with Meatballs

Serves 6-8

INGREDIENTS

200 g/7 oz/1¹/2 cups *masoor dhaal*
1 tsp fresh ginger root, crushed
1 tsp fresh garlic, crushed
¹/2 tsp turmeric
1¹/2 tsp chilli powder
1¹/2 tsp salt
3 tbsp lemon juice

850 ml/1¹/2 pints/3³/4 cups water

BAGHAAR:
150 ml/¹/4 pint/²/3 cup oil
3 garlic cloves
4 dried red chillies
1 tsp white cumin seeds

POTATO FRIES:
pinch of salt
2 medium potatoes, sliced
300 ml/¹/2 pint/1¹/4 cups oil

1 Rinse the lentils, removing any stones, then place them in a pan and cover with 600 ml/1 pint/2¹/2 cups water. Add the ginger, garlic, turmeric and chilli powder and boil until the lentils are mushy. Add the salt, stirring.

2 Mash the lentils, then push them through a sieve, reserving the liquid. Add the lemon juice to the strained liquid.

3 Stir 300 ml/¹/2 pint/1¹/4 cups of water into the strained liquid and boil over a low heat. Set aside.

4 To make the meatballs, follow the recipe for Beef Kebabs (Kabobs) on page 46 but use the reserved strained liquid instead of water and shape the mixture into small balls rather than flat rounds. Drop the meatballs gently into the lentil mixture.

5 To make the *baghaar*, fry the garlic, dried red chillies and white cumin seeds in a pan of heated oil for 2 minutes. Pour over the lentil mixture, stirring.

6 For the potato fries, rub the salt over the potato slices and fry in oil in a frying pan (skillet) until crisp. Garnish the meatballs with the fried potatoes and serve immediately.

Spiced Rice & Lentils

Serves 4

INGREDIENTS

200 g/7 oz/1 cup basmati rice
175 g/6 oz/¾ cup *masoor dhaal*
2 tbsp pure or vegetable ghee

1 small onion, sliced
1 tsp fresh ginger root, finely chopped

1 tsp fresh garlic, crushed
½ tsp turmeric
600 ml/1 pint/2½ cups water
1 tsp salt

1 Combine the rice and *dhaal* and rinse twice, rubbing with your fingers, and removing any stones. Set aside until required.

2 Heat the ghee in a large saucepan. Add the onion and fry, stirring occasionally, for about 2 minutes.

3 Reduce the heat, add the ginger, garlic, and turmeric and stir-fry for 1 minute.

4 Add the rice and *dhaal* to the mixture in the pan and mix gently.

5 Add the water to the mixture in the pan and bring to the boil. Reduce the heat and cook, covered, for 20-25 minutes.

6 Just before serving, add the salt and mix well to combine.

7 Transfer the spiced rice and lentils to a serving dish and serve immediately.

VARIATION

Moong dhaal *may be substituted for* masoor dhaal *in this recipe.*

COOK'S TIP

Many Indian recipes specify using ghee as the cooking fat. This is because it is similar to clarified butter in that it can be heated to a very high temperature without burning. Ghee adds a nutty flavour to dishes and a glossy shine to sauces. You can buy ghee in cans, and a vegetarian version is also available. Store at room temperature or keep in the refrigerator.

Chana Dhaal Cooked with Rice

Serves 6

INGREDIENTS

100 g/3½ oz/¾ cup *chana dhaal*
450 g/1 lb/2¼ cups basmati rice
60 ml/4 tbsp ghee
2 medium onions, finely sliced
1 tsp fresh ginger root, finely chopped

1 tsp fresh garlic, crushed
½ tsp turmeric
2 tsp salt
½ tsp chilli powder
1 tsp garam masala
5 tbsp yogurt
1.35 litres/2¼ pints/5⅔ cups water

150 ml/¼ pint/⅔ cup milk
1 tsp saffron
3 tbsp lemon juice
2 green chillies, sliced
fresh coriander (cilantro) leaves, chopped
3 black cardamoms
3 black cumin seeds

1 Rinse and soak the *chana dhaal* for 3 hours. Rinse the rice, removing any stones and set aside.

2 Heat the ghee in a frying pan (skillet). Add the onion and fry until golden. Remove half of the onion plus a little ghee with a perforated spoon and set aside in a bowl.

3 Add the ginger, garlic, turmeric, 1 tsp of salt, the chilli powder and garam masala to the onions in the pan and fry for 5 minutes. Stir in the yogurt, add the *chana dhaal* and 150 ml/¼ pint /⅔ cup water. Cook, covered, for 15 minutes.

4 Meanwhile, boil the milk with the saffron and set aside with the reserved fried onion, lemon juice, green chillies and coriander (cilantro) leaves.

5 Boil the rest of the water and add the salt, black cardamoms, black cumin seeds and the rice, and cook, stirring, until the rice is half-cooked. Drain, and place half of the fried onion, saffron and green chilli mixture on top of the *chana dhaal*. Place the remaining rice on top of this and the rest of the fried onion mixture on top of the rice. Cover tightly with a lid and cook for 20 minutes over a very low heat. Mix with a slotted spoon before serving.

Pulao Rice

Serves 2-4

INGREDIENTS

200 g/7 oz/1 cup basmati rice
2 tbsp ghee
3 green cardamoms
2 cloves

3 peppercorns
1/2 tsp salt
1/2 tsp saffron

400 ml/3/4 pint/2 cups water

1 Rinse the rice twice and set aside in a bowl until required.

2 Heat the ghee in a saucepan. Add the cardamoms, cloves and peppercorns to the pan and fry, stirring, for about 1 minute.

3 Add the rice and stir-fry for a further 2 minutes.

4 Add the salt, saffron and water to the rice mixture and reduce the heat. Cover the pan and leave to simmer over a low heat until the water has evaporated.

5 Transfer to a serving dish and serve hot.

COOK'S TIP

Cloves should be used with caution because the flavour can be overwhelming if too many are used.

COOK'S TIP

The most expensive of all spices, saffron strands are the stamens of a type of crocus. They give dishes a rich, golden colour, as well as adding a distinctive, slightly bitter taste. Saffron is sold as a powder or in strands. Saffron strands are more expensive, but do have a superior flavour. Some books recommend substituting turmeric – although the colours are similar, the tastes are not.

Fried Spicy Rice

Serves 4–6

INGREDIENTS

450 g/1 lb/2¼ cups rice
1 medium onion
2 tbsp ghee
1 tsp fresh ginger root, finely
    chopped

1 tsp fresh garlic, crushed
1 tsp salt
1 tsp black cumin seeds
3 whole cloves

3 whole green cardamoms
2 cinnamon sticks
4 peppercorns
750 ml/1¼ pints/3¼ cups
    water

1 Rinse the rice, removing any stones.

2 Using a sharp knife, slice the onion.

3 Melt the ghee in a large saucepan and fry the onion until a crisp golden brown colour.

4 Add the ginger, garlic and salt to the onions in the pan, stirring well to combine.

5 Remove half of the spicy onions from the saucepan and set aside.

6 Add the rice, black cumin seeds, cloves, cardamoms, cinnamon sticks and peppercorns to the mixture in the pan and stir-fry for 3–5 minutes.

7 Add the water to the mixture in the pan and bring to the boil. Reduce the heat, cover and cook until steam comes out of the lid. Check to see whether the rice is cooked.

8 Transfer the fried spicy rice to a serving dish and serve garnished with the reserved fried onions.

COOK'S TIP

Cardamom pods contain numerous tiny black seeds which have a warm flavour and are highly aromatic – green cardamoms are considered the best because of their fine delicate flavour. Green cardamoms are also prized for their digestive properties, and some Indians chew them raw after they have eaten extra-spicy curries, to aid digestion and sweeten the breath.

Vegetable Pulao

Serves 4-6

INGREDIENTS

2 medium potatoes, each
   peeled and cut into 6
1 medium aubergine
   (eggplant), cut into 6
200 g/7 oz carrots, peeled and
   sliced
50 g/1¾ oz green beans, cut
   into pieces
4 tbsp ghee
2 medium onions, sliced
175 ml/6 fl oz/¾ cup yogurt

2 tsp fresh ginger root, finely
   chopped
2 tsp fresh garlic, crushed
2 tsp garam masala
2 tsp black cumin seeds
½ tsp turmeric
3 black cardamoms
3 cinnamon sticks
2 tsp salt
1 tsp chilli powder

½ tsp saffron strands
300 ml/½ pint/1¼ cups milk
600 g/1½ lb/3 cups basmati
   rice
5 tbsp lemon juice

1 Prepare the vegetables. Heat the ghee in a pan (skillet) and fry the potatoes, aubergine (eggplant), carrots and beans, stirring. Remove from the pan and set aside. Fry the onions until soft and add the yogurt, ginger, garlic, garam masala, 1 tsp black cumin seeds, turmeric, 1 cardamom, 1 cinnamon stick, 1 tsp salt and the chilli powder and stir-fry for 3-5 minutes. Return the vegetables to the pan and fry for 4-5 minutes.

2 Boil the saffron strands in the milk, stirring. In a pan of boiling water, half-cook the rice with 1 tsp salt, 2 cinnamon sticks, 2 black cardamoms and 1 tsp black cumin seeds. Drain the rice, leaving half in the pan while transferring the other half to a bowl. Pour the vegetable mixture on top of the rice in the pan. Pour half of the lemon juice and half the saffron in milk over the vegetables and rice, cover with the remaining rice and lemon juice and saffron in milk. Cover and cook over a low heat for 20 minutes. Serve hot.

Brown Rice with Fruit & Nuts

Serves 4-6

INGREDIENTS

4 tbsp vegetable ghee or oil	300 g/10 oz/1^1/2 cups brown	1 red (bell) pepper, cored,
1 large onion, chopped	rice	seeded and diced
2 garlic cloves, crushed	850 ml/1^1/2 pints/3^1/2 cups	90 g/3 oz frozen peas
2.5 cm/1 inch ginger root,	boiling vegetable stock	1-2 small, slightly green
chopped finely	400 g/14 oz can chopped	bananas
1 tsp chilli powder	tomatoes	60-90 g/2-3oz/^{1}/3-^{1}/2 cup
1 tsp cumin seeds	175 g/6 oz ready-soaked dried	toasted mixed nuts
1 tbsp mild or medium curry	apricots or peaches, cut	salt and pepper
powder or paste	into slivers	

1 Heat the ghee or oil in a large saucepan, add the onion and fry gently for 3 minutes.

2 Stir in the garlic, ginger, chilli powder, cumin seeds, curry powder or paste and rice. Cook gently for 2 minutes, stirring, until the rice is coated in the spiced oil.

3 Pour in the boiling stock, stirring to mix.

Add the tomatoes and season with salt and pepper. Bring to the boil, then reduce the heat, cover and leave to simmer gently for 40 minutes or until the rice is almost cooked and most of the liquid is absorbed.

4 Add the apricots or peaches, red (bell) pepper and peas to the rice mixture in the pan. Cover and continue cooking for 10 minutes.

5 Remove the pan from the heat and leave to stand for 5 minutes without uncovering.

6 Peel and slice the bananas. Uncover the rice mixture and toss with a fork to mix. Add the toasted nuts and sliced banana and toss lightly.

7 Transfer the rice dish to a serving platter and serve hot.

Prawn (Shrimp) Pulao

Serves 4

INGREDIENTS

450 g/1 lb frozen prawns
   (shrimp)
$^1/_2$ tsp saffron
150 ml/$^1/_2$ pint/1$^1/_4$ cups milk
1 tsp chilli powder
1$^1/_2$ tsp caraway seeds

2 cinnamon sticks
2 green cardamoms
2 medium onions, sliced
2 bay leaves
1 tsp fresh ginger root, finely
   chopped
5 ml/1 tsp salt

450 g/1 lb/2$^1/_4$ cups basmati
   rice
5 tbsp ghee
4 tbsp lemon juice
fresh mint leaves, plus extra to
   garnish

1 Defrost the prawns by placing them in a bowl of cold water.

2 Boil 150 ml/$^1/_4$ pint/ $^2/_3$ cup of the milk in a pan and add the saffron. Set aside until required.

3 Place the chilli powder, 1 tsp caraway seeds, cinnamon sticks, green cardamoms, 1 sliced onion, the bay leaves, ginger and salt in a pestle and mortar and grind to a fine paste. Set aside.

4 Place the rice in a saucepan of boiling water and when the rice is half-cooked, remove from the heat and set aside.

5 Heat the ghee in a pan and fry the remaining onion until golden brown. Transfer to a bowl and mix with the lemon juice and a few mint leaves.

6 Add the spice paste and prawns (shrimps) to the pan and stir-fry for about 5 minutes. Remove the prawns (shrimps) and spices and place in a bowl.

7 Place the half-cooked rice in a saucepan and pour the prawn (shrimp) mixture on top. Add half of the onion mixture and half of the saffron mixture. Arrange the remaining rice on top and pour over the remaining ingredients. Add the extra mint leaves, cover and cook over a low heat for 15-20 minutes. Mix well before arranging in a serving dish.

Chicken Biryani

Serves 6

INGREDIENTS

$1^{1}/_2$ tsp fresh ginger root, finely chopped
$1^{1}/_2$ tsp fresh garlic, crushed
1 tbsp garam masala
1 tsp chilli powder
$1/_2$ tsp turmeric
2 tsp salt
20 crushed green/white cardamom seeds, crushed

300 ml/10 fl oz/$1^{1}/_4$ cups natural yogurt
1.5 kg/3 lb 5 oz chicken, skinned and cut into 8
150 ml/$1/_4$ pint/$2/_3$ cup milk
$1/_2$ tsp saffron strands
6 tbsp ghee
2 medium onions, sliced

450 g/1 lb/$2^{1}/_4$ cups basmati rice
1 tsp black cumin seeds
2 cinnamon sticks
4 black peppercorns
4 green chillies
fresh coriander (cilantro) leaves, finely chopped
4 tbsp lemon juice

1 Blend together the ginger, garlic, garam masala, chilli powder, turmeric, 1 tsp salt and cardamom seeds and mix with the yogurt and chicken pieces. Set aside to marinate for 3 hours.

2 Boil the milk in a pan, pour over the saffron and set aside.

3 Heat the ghee in a pan and fry the onions until golden. Remove half of the onions and ghee from the pan and set aside.

4 Place the rice in a pan with twice as much water as rice. Add the cumin, cinnamon and peppercorns. Boil until half-cooked. Drain, place in a bowl and mix with the rest of the salt.

5 Finely chop all of the green chillies.

6 Add the chicken mixture to the pan containing the onions and ghee. Add half each of the green chillies, coriander (cilantro), lemon juice and saffron milk. Add the rice and then the rest of the ingredients, including the onions and ghee. Cover tightly and cook on a low heat for about 1 hour. If the meat is not cooked through, cook for a further 15 minutes. Serve at once.

Tomato Rice

Serves 4

INGREDIENTS

150 ml/^{1}/$_4$ pint/^{2}/$_3$ cup oil
2 medium onions, sliced
1 tsp onion seeds
1 tsp fresh ginger root, finely
    chopped
1 tsp fresh garlic, crushed
^{1}/$_2$ tsp turmeric

1 tsp chilli powder
1^1/$_2$ tsp salt
400 g/14 oz can tomatoes
450 g/1 lb/2^1/$_4$ cups basmati
    rice
600 ml/1 pint/2^1/$_2$ cups water

3 fresh green chillies, finely
    chopped, to garnish

1 Heat the oil in a saucepan and fry the onions until golden brown.

2 Add the onion seeds, ginger, garlic, turmeric, chilli powder and salt, stirring to combine.

3 Reduce the heat, add the tomatoes and stir-fry for 10 minutes.

4 Add the rice to the tomato mixture, stirring gently, to coat the rice in the mixture.

5 Pour in the water, stirring to incorporate. Cover the pan and cook over a low heat until the water has been absorbed and the rice is cooked.

6 Transfer the tomato rice to a serving dish.

7 Garnish with the finely chopped green chillies. Serve the tomato rice dish immediately.

COOK'S TIP

Onion seeds are always used whole in Indian cooking. They are often used in pickles and often sprinkled over the top of Naan Breads (see page 178). Ironically, onion seeds don't have anything to do with the vegetable, but they look similar to the plant's seed, hence the name.

Lamb Biryani

Serves 4-6

INGREDIENTS

150 ml/¹/₄ pint/²/₃ cup milk
1 tsp saffron
5 tbsp ghee
3 medium onions, sliced
1 kg/2 lb 5 oz lean lamb, cubed
7 tbsp natural yogurt
1¹/₂ tsp fresh ginger root,
   finely chopped

1¹/₂ tsp fresh garlic, crushed
2 tsp garam masala
2 tsp salt
¹/₄ tsp turmeric
600 ml/1 pint/2¹/₂ cups water
450 g/1 lb/2¹/₄ cups basmati
   rice
2 tsp black cumin seeds

3 cardamoms
4 tbsp lemon juice
2 fresh green chillies
¹/₄ bunch fresh coriander
   (cilantro) leaves

1 Boil the milk in a pan with the saffron and set aside. Heat the ghee in a pan and fry the onions until golden. Remove half of the onions and ghee from the pan and set aside.

2 Combine the meat, yogurt, ginger, garlic, garam masala, 1 tsp salt and turmeric in a large bowl.

3 Return the pan with the ghee and onions to the heat, add the meat mixture, stir for 3 minutes and add the water. Cook on a low heat for 45 minutes, stirring occasionally. If the meat is not tender, add 150 ml/¹/₄ pint/²/₃ cup water and cook for 15 minutes. Once the water has evaporated, stir-fry for 2 minutes and set aside.

4 Meanwhile, place the rice in a pan. Add the cumin seeds, cardamoms, salt and enough water for cooking, and cook over a medium heat until the rice is half-cooked. Drain. Remove half of the rice.

5 Spoon the meat mixture on top of the rice in the pan. Add half each of the saffron milk, lemon juice, chillies and coriander (cilantro). Add the reserved onion and ghee mixture, the other half of the rice and other ingredients. Cover and cook over a low heat for 15-20 minutes. Serve hot.

Paratas stuffed with Vegetables

Makes 4-6

INGREDIENTS

DOUGH:
225 g/8 oz/1³/₄ cups
    wholemeal flour (*ata* or
    chapati flour)
¹/₂ tsp salt
200 ml/¹/₃ pint/³/₄ cup water

100 g/3¹/₂ oz/8 tbsp pure or
    vegetable ghee
2 tbsp ghee, for frying

FILLING:
3 medium potatoes
¹/₂ tsp turmeric

1 tsp garam masala
1 tsp fresh ginger root, finely
    chopped
fresh coriander (cilantro)
    leaves
3 green chillies, finely chopped
1 tsp salt

1 To make the *paratas*, mix the flour, salt, water and ghee in a bowl to form a dough.

2 Divide the dough into 6-8 equal portions. Roll each portion out on to a floured work surface. Brush the middle of each portion with ¹/₂ tsp ghee. Fold the portions in half, roll into a pipe-like shape, flatten with the palms of your hands, then roll around your finger to form a coil. Roll out again, using flour to dust, to form a round 18 cm/7 inches in diameter.

3 Place the potatoes in a saucepan of water and cook until soft enough to be mashed.

4 Blend the turmeric, garam masala, ginger, coriander (cilantro), chillies and salt together in a bowl.

5 Add the spice mixture to the mashed potato and mix well. Spread about 1 tbsp of the spicy potato mixture on each dough portion and cover with another rolled-out piece of dough. Seal the edges well.

6 Heat 2 tsp ghee in a heavy-bottomed frying-pan (skillet). Place the *paratas* gently in the pan in batches and fry, turning and moving them about gently with a flat spoon, until golden. Remove the *paratas* from the frying pan (skillet) and serve immediately.

Gram Flour Bread

Makes 4-6

INGREDIENTS

100 g/3¹/2 oz/³/4 cup
wholemeal flour (ata or
chapati flour)
75 g/2³/4 oz/¹/2 cup gram
flour

¹/2 tsp salt
1 small onion
fresh coriander (cilantro)
leaves, chopped very finely

2 fresh green chillies, chopped
very finely
150 ml/¹/4 pint/²/3 cup water
2 tsp ghee

1 Sift the wholemeal and gram flours together in a large mixing bowl. Add the salt to the flour and mix to combine.

2 Using a sharp knife, peel and chop the onion very finely.

3 Blend the onion, chopped coriander (cilantro) and chillies into the flour mixture.

4 Add the water and mix to form a soft dough. Cover the dough and set aside for about 15 minutes.

5 Knead the dough for 5-7 minutes.

6 Divide the dough into 8 equal portions.

7 Roll out the dough portions to about 18 cm/7 inches on a lightly floured surface.

8 Place the dough portions individually in a frying-pan (skillet) and cook over a medium heat, turning three times and lightly greasing each side with the ghee each time. Transfer the gram

flour bread to serving plates and serve hot.

COOK'S TIP

Also called besan flour, gram flour is a pale yellow flour made from ground chick-peas (garbanzo beans). In Indian kitchens it is used to make breads, bhajis and batters and to thicken sauces and stabilize yogurt when it is added to hot dishes. Buy it from Indian food stores or large health food stores and store in a cool, dark place in an air-tight container.

Naan Bread

Makes 6–8

INGREDIENTS

1 tsp sugar
1 tsp fresh yeast
150 ml/^{1}/$_4$ pint/^{2}/$_3$ cup warm
   water

200 g/7 oz/1^1/$_2$ cups plain (all-
   purpose) flour
1 tbsp ghee

1 tsp salt
50 g/1^3/$_4$ oz/6 tbsp unsalted
   butter
1 tsp poppy seeds

1 Put the sugar and yeast in a small bowl or jug with the warm water and mix well until the yeast has dissolved. Set aside for about 10 minutes or until the mixture is frothy.

2 Place the flour in a large mixing bowl. Make a well in the middle of the flour, add the ghee and salt and pour in the yeast mixture. Mix well to form a dough, using your hands and adding more water if required.

3 Turn the dough out on to a floured surface and knead for 5 minutes or until smooth.

4 Return the dough to the bowl, cover and leave to rise in a warm place for 1½ hours or until doubled in size.

5 Turn the dough out on to a floured surface and knead for a further 2 minutes. Break off small balls with your hand and pat them into rounds about 12 cm/5 inches in diameter and 1 cm/½ inch thick.

6 Place the dough rounds on to a greased sheet of foil and grill (broil) under a very hot pre-heated grill (broiler) for 7–10 minutes, turning twice and brushing with the butter and sprinkling with the poppy seeds.

7 Serve warm immediately, or keep wrapped in foil until required.

Chapati

Makes 10–12

INGREDIENTS

225 g/8 oz/1¹/₂ cups wholemeal flour (*ata* or *chapati* flour)

¹/₂ tsp salt

200 ml/¹/₃ pint/³/₄ cup water

1 Place the flour in a large mixing bowl. Add the salt and mix well to combine.

2 Make a well in the middle of the flour and gradually pour in the water, mixing well with your fingers to form a supple dough.

3 Knead the dough for about 7–10 minutes. Ideally, set the dough aside and leave to rise for about 15–20 minutes, but if time is short roll out the dough straightaway. Divide the dough into 10–12 equal portions. Roll out each piece of dough to form a round on a well-floured surface.

4 Place a heavy-based frying-pan (skillet) on a high heat. When steam starts to rise from the frying pan (skillet), lower the heat to medium.

5 Place a chapati in the frying pan (skillet) and when the chapati starts to bubble turn it over. Carefully press down on the chapati with a clean tea towel (dishcloth) or a flat spoon and turn the chapati over once again. Remove the chapati from the pan, set aside and keep warm while you make the others.

6 Repeat the process until all of the chapatis are cooked.

COOK'S TIP

Ideally, chapatis should be eaten as they come out of the frying pan (skillet), but if that is not practical keep them warm after cooking by wrapping them up in foil.
In India, chapatis are sometimes cooked on a naked flame, which makes them puff up. Allow about 2 per person.

Lightly Fried Bread

Makes 10

INGREDIENTS

225 g/8 oz/1 1/2 cups wholemeal flour (*ata* or *chapati* flour)	1/2 tsp salt 1 tbsp ghee	300 ml/1/2 pint/1 1/4 cups water

1 Place the wholemeal flour (*ata* or *chapati* flour) and the salt in a large mixing bowl and mix to combine.

2 Make a well in the middle of the flour. Add the ghee and rub in well. Gradually pour in the water and work to form a soft dough. Set the dough aside to rise for about 10-15 minutes.

3 Carefully knead the risen dough with your hands for 5-7 minutes. Then divide the dough into about 10 equal portions, ready for rolling.

4 On a lightly floured surface, roll out each dough portion to form a flat pancake shape.

5 Using a sharp knife, lightly draw lines in a criss-cross pattern on each dough portion.

6 Heat a heavy-bottomed frying pan (skillet). Gently place the dough portions, one by one, into the pan.

7 Cook the bread for about 1 minute, then turn over and spread with 1 tsp ghee. Turn the bread over again and fry gently, moving it around the pan with a spatula, until golden. Turn the bread over once again, then remove from the pan and keep warm while you cook the remaining batches.

COOK'S TIP

In India, breads are cooked on a tava, *a traditional flat griddle. A large frying pan (skillet) makes an adequate substitute.*

Poori

Makes 10

| INGREDIENTS |

225 g/8 oz/1 1/2 cups
wholemeal flour (*ata* or
chapati flour)

1/2 tsp salt
150 ml/1/4 pint/2/3 cup water

600 ml/1 pint/2 1/2 cups oil

1 Place the flour and salt in a large mixing bowl and stir to combine.

2 Make a well in the centre of the flour. Gradually pour in the water and mix together to form a dough, adding more water if necessary.

3 Knead the dough until it is smooth and elastic and leave in a warm place to rise for 15 minutes.

4 Divide the dough into about 10 equal portions and with lightly oiled or floured hands pat each into a smooth ball.

5 On a lightly oiled or floured surface, roll out each dough ball to form a thin round.

6 Heat the oil in a deep frying-pan (skillet). Deep-fry the rounds in batches, turning once, until golden in colour.

7 Remove the *pooris* from the pan and drain. Serve hot.

COOK'S TIP

You can serve pooris either piled one on top of the other or spread out in a layer on a large serving platter so that they remain puffed up.

COOK'S TIP

You can make pooris in advance, if you prefer. Wrap in kitchen foil and reheat in a hot oven for about 10 minutes when required.

Snacks & Side Dishes

In India, we like having tea parties at
about 5 or 6 o'clock in the evening, especially in
the month of Ramadan, when people meet after
fasting all day, and we serve little snacks such as the
ones in this chapter. They are ideal for cocktail or
other drinks parties, when you would like to offer
something more interesting than the usual peanuts
and crisps. The basic quantities are for 4 people,
but you can multiply according to the
number on your guest list.

Accompaniments – a simple Carrot
Salad or a Mint Raita, for example – always
add colour and variety to a meal. Most take very
little time to prepare, but taste delicious. None of
these accompaniments has to be made in large
quantities, because they are only taken in small
amounts: variety is better than quantity!

Fried Aubergines (Eggplants) in Yogurt

Serves 4

INGREDIENTS

200 ml/7 fl oz/³/4 cup natural yogurt	1 tsp salt	150 ml/¹/4 pint/²/3 cup oil
75 ml/3 fl oz/¹/3 cup water	1 medium aubergine (eggplant)	1 tsp white cumin seeds
		6 dried red chillies

1 Place the yogurt in a bowl and whip with a fork.

2 Add the water and salt to the yogurt and mix together well. Transfer to a serving bowl.

3 Using a sharp knife, slice the aubergine (eggplant) thinly.

4 Heat the oil in a large frying-pan (skillet). Add the aubergine (eggplant) slices and fry, in batches, over a medium heat, turning occasionally,

until they begin to turn crisp. Remove from the pan, transfer to a serving plate and keep warm.

5 When all of the aubergine (eggplant) slices have been fried, lower the heat, and add the white cumin seeds and the dried red chillies to the pan. Cook for 1 minute, stirring.

6 Spoon the yogurt on top of the aubergines (eggplants), then pour over the white cumin and red chilli mixture. Serve immediately.

VARIATION

Finely chop and deseed the dried red chillies, if you prefer.

COOK'S TIP

Rich in protein and calcium, yogurt plays an important part in Indian cooking. It is used as a marinade, as a creamy flavouring in curries and sauces and as a cooling accompaniment to hot dishes.

Spicy Corn

Serves 4

INGREDIENTS
---

200 g/7 oz/1 cup canned or
    frozen sweetcorn
1 tsp ground cumin
1 tsp fresh garlic, crushed

1 tsp ground coriander
1 tsp salt
2 fresh green chillies
1 medium onion, finely
    chopped

3 tbsp unsalted butter
4 red chillies, crushed
$1/2$ tsp lemon juice
fresh coriander (cilantro)
    leaves, chopped, to garnish

1 Thaw (frozen) or drain (canned) the sweetcorn and set aside.

2 Place the ground cumin, garlic, ground coriander, salt, 1 fresh green chilli and the onion in a pestle and mortar or a food processor and grind to form a smooth paste.

3 Heat the butter in a large frying pan (skillet). Add the onion and spice mixture to the pan and fry over a medium heat, stirring occasionally, for about 5-7 minutes.

4 Add the crushed red chillies to the pan and stir to mix.

5 Add the sweetcorn to the pan and stir-fry for a further 2 minutes.

6 Add the remaining green chilli, lemon juice and the fresh coriander (cilantro) leaves to the pan, stirring occasionally to combine.

7 Transfer to a warm serving dish. Garnish with fresh coriander (cilantro) and serve hot.

COOK'S TIP

Coriander is available ground or as seeds and is one of the essential ingredients in Indian cooking. Coriander seeds are often dry roasted before use to develop their flavour.

Pakoras

Serves 4

INGREDIENTS

6 tbsp gram flour
1/2 tsp salt
1 tsp chilli powder
1 tsp baking powder
11/2 tsp white cumin seeds

1 tsp pomegranate seeds
300 ml/1/2 pint/11/4 cups
   water
fresh coriander (cilantro)
   leaves, finely chopped

vegetables of your choice:
   cauliflower, cut into small
   florets, onions, cut into
   rings, potatoes, sliced,
   aubergines (eggplants),
   sliced, or fresh spinach
   leaves)
oil, for deep-frying

1 Sift the gram flour into a large mixing bowl.

2 Add the salt, chilli powder, baking powder, cumin and pomegranate seeds and blend together well.

3 Pour in the water and beat well to form a smooth batter.

4 Add the coriander (cilantro) and mix. Set the batter aside.

5 Dip the prepared vegetables of your choice into the batter, carefully shaking off any of the excess batter.

6 Heat the oil in a large heavy-based pan. Place the battered vegetables of your choice in the oil and deep-fry, in batches, turning once.

7 Repeat this process until all of the batter has been used up.

8 Transfer the battered vegetables to kitchen paper and drain. Serve immediately.

COOK'S TIP

When deep-frying, it is important to use oil at the correct temperature. If it is too hot, the outside of the food will burn before the inside is cooked. If too cool, the food will be sodden with oil before a batter forms.

Indian-Style Omelette

Serves 2-4

INGREDIENTS

1 small onion, very finely chopped	fresh coriander (cilantro) leaves, finely chopped	1 tsp salt
2 green chillies, finely chopped	4 medium eggs	2 tbsp oil

1 Place the onion, chillies and coriander (cilantro) in a large mixing bowl. Mix together, ideally with your fingers.

2 Place the eggs in a separate bowl and whisk together.

3 Add the onion mixture to the eggs and mix together well.

4 Add the salt to the egg and onion mixture and whisk together well.

5 Heat 1 tbsp of the oil in a large frying pan (skillet). Place a ladleful of the omelette batter into the heated pan.

6 Fry the omelette, turning once and pressing down with a flat spoon to make sure that the egg is cooked right through, until the omelette is a golden brown colour.

7 Repeat the same process for the remaining batter. Set the omelettes aside and keep warm while you make the remaining batches of omelettes.

8 Serve the omelettes immediately with Paratas (see page 174) or toasted bread. Alternatively, simply serve the omelettes with a crisp green salad for a light lunch.

COOK'S TIP

Indian cooks use a variety of vegetable oils, and groundnut or sunflower oils make good alternatives for most dishes, although sometimes more specialist ones, such as coconut oil, mustard oil and sesame oil, are called for.

Samosas

Makes 10-12

INGREDIENTS

PASTRY:
100 g/3¹/2 oz/³/4 cup self-
    raising flour
¹/2 tsp salt
40 g/1¹/2 oz/3 tbsp butter, cut
    into small pieces
4 tbsp water

FILLING:
3 medium potatoes, boiled
1 tsp fresh ginger root, finely
    chopped
1 tsp fresh garlic, crushed
¹/2 tsp white cumin seeds
¹/2 tsp mixed onion and
    mustard seeds

1 tsp salt
¹/2 tsp crushed red chillies
2 tbsp lemon juice
2 small green chillies, finely
    chopped
ghee or oil, for deep-frying

1 Sift the flour and salt into a large mixing bowl. Add the butter and rub into the flour until the mixture resembles fine breadcrumbs.

2 Pour in the water and mix with a fork to form a dough. Pat the dough into a ball and knead for 5 minutes or until the dough is smooth. Add a little flour if the dough is sticky. Cover and leave to rise.

3 To make the filling, mash the boiled potatoes gently and mix with the ginger, garlic, white cumin seeds, onion and mustard seeds, salt, crushed red chillies, lemon juice and green chillies.

4 Break small balls off the dough and roll each out very thinly to form a round. Cut in half, dampen the edges and shape into cones. Fill the cones with a little of the filling, dampen the top and bottom edges of the cones and pinch together to seal. Set aside.

5 Fill a deep pan one-third full with oil; heat to 180°-190°C/350°-375°F or until a cube of bread browns in 30 seconds. Carefully lower the samosas into the oil, a few at a time, and fry until golden brown. Remove and drain on kitchen towels. Serve hot or cold.

Chick-Pea (Garbanzo Bean) Snack

Serves 2-4

INGREDIENTS

400 g/14 oz can chick-peas
(garbanzo beans), drained
2 medium potatoes
1 medium onion
2 tbsp tamarind paste

6 tbsp water
1 tsp chilli powder
2 tsp sugar
1 tsp salt

TO GARNISH:
1 tomato, sliced
2 fresh green chillies, chopped
fresh coriander (cilantro)
leaves

1 Place the drained chick-peas (garbanzo beans) in a bowl.

2 Using a sharp knife, dice the potatoes.

3 Place the diced potatoes in a saucepan of water and boil until cooked through. Test by inserting the tip of a knife into the potatoes – they should feel soft and tender. Set aside until required.

4 Using a sharp knife, finely chop the onion. Set aside until required.

5 Mix together the tamarind paste and water in a small mixing bowl.

6 Add the chilli powder, sugar and salt to the tamarind paste mixture and mix together. Pour the mixture over the chick-peas (garbanzo beans).

7 Add the onion and the diced potatoes, and stir to mix. Season to taste with a little salt.

8 Transfer to a serving bowl and garnish with tomatoes, chillies and coriander (cilantro) leaves.

COOK'S TIP

Cream-coloured and resembling a hazelnut in appearance, chick-peas (garbanzo breans) have a nutty flavour and slightly crunchy texture. Indian cooks also grind these to make a flour called gram or besan, which is used to make breads, thicken sauces, and to make batters for deep-fried dishes.

Soft Dumplings in Yogurt with Masala

Serves 4

INGREDIENTS

200 g/7 oz/1^1/$_2$ cups *urid dhaal* powder
1 tsp baking powder
^{1}/$_2$ tsp ground ginger
300 ml/^{1}/$_2$ pint/1^1/$_4$ cups water
oil, for deep-frying

400 ml/15 fl oz/1^3/$_4$ cups natural yogurt
75 g/2^3/$_4$ oz/5 tbsp sugar

MASALA:
50 g/1^3/$_4$ oz/6 tbsp ground coriander

50 g/1^3/$_4$ oz/6 tbsp ground white cumin
25 g/1 oz crushed red chillies
100 g/3^1/$_2$ oz/^{1}/$_2$ cup citric acid
chopped red chillies, to garnish

1 Place the powdered *urid dhaal* in a large mixing bowl. Add the baking powder and ground ginger and stir to combine. Add the water and mix to form a paste.

2 Heat the oil in a deep pan or frying pan (skillet). Pour in the batter, 1 tsp at a time, and deep-fry the dumplings until golden brown, lowering the heat when the oil gets too hot. Set the dumplings aside.

3 Place the yogurt in a separate bowl. Add 400 ml/15 fl oz/1^3/$_4$ cups water and the sugar and mix together with a whisk or fork. Set aside.

4 To make the *masala*, roast the ground coriander and the white cumin in a saucepan until a little darker in colour. Grind coarsely in a food processor or pestle and mortar. Add the crushed red chillies and citric acid and blend well together.

5 Sprinkle about 1 tbsp of the *masala* over the dumplings and garnish with chopped red chillies. Serve with the reserved yogurt mixture.

COOK'S TIP

The masala *(spice mixture) for the dumplings is usually made in a large quantity as it can be stored in an airtight container.*

Spiced Semolina

Serves 4

INGREDIENTS

150 ml/¹/₄ pint/²/₃ cup oil
1 tsp mixed onion and
      mustard seeds
4 dried red chillies

4 curry leaves (fresh or dried)
8 tbsp coarse semolina
50 g/1³/₄ oz cashew nuts

1 tsp salt
150 ml/¹/₄ pint/²/₃ cup water

1 Heat the oil in a large, heavy frying-pan (skillet).

2 Add the mixed onion and mustard seeds, dried red chillies and curry leaves and stir-fry for about 1 minute, stirring constantly.

3 Reduce the heat and add the coarse semolina and the cashew nuts to the mixture in the pan. Quickly stir-fry for about 5 minutes, moving the mixture around the pan all the time so that it does not catch and burn on the bottom of the pan.

4 Add the salt to the mixture and continue to stir-fry, stirring constantly.

5 Add the water and cook, stirring continuously, until the mixture starts to thicken.

6 Serve the spiced semolina warm as a teatime snack.

COOK'S TIP

The basic quantity here is for 4 people, which you can multiply according to your guest list.

COOK'S TIP

Curry leaves are very similar in appearance to bay leaves but are very different in flavour. They can be bought both fresh and dried. They are mainly used to flavour lentil dishes and vegetable curries.

Sweet & Sour Fruit

Serves 4

INGREDIENTS

400 g/14 oz can mixed fruit cocktail	3 apples	2 tbsp lemon juice
400 g/14 oz can guavas	1 tsp ground black pepper	1/2 tsp ground ginger
2 large bananas	1 tsp salt	fresh mint leaves, to garnish

1 Drain the can of fruit cocktail and pour the fruit pieces into a deep mixing bowl.

2 Mix the guavas and their syrup with the drained fruit cocktail.

3 Peel the bananas and cut into slices.

4 Peel and core the apples (optional) and cut into dice.

5 Add the pieces of fresh fruit to the bowl containing the canned fruit and mix together.

6 Add the ground black pepper, salt, lemon juice and ginger and stir well to mix.

7 Serve as a snack garnished with a few fresh mint leaves.

COOK'S TIP

The lemon juice in this recipe serves to add a sharp flavour to the dish but it also prevents the banana and apple from dicolouring and turning brown when the flesh is exposed to the air.

COOK'S TIP

Ginger is one of the most popular spices in India and also one of the oldest. It can be bought as fresh ginger root in most large supermarkets. It should always be peeled before use and can be finely chopped or puréed. Ground ginger is also useful to have in your storecupboard.

Mixed Rice, Nuts & Raisins

Serves 4

INGREDIENTS
---

50 g/1³/₄ oz/¹/₃ cup *chana dhaal*

300 ml/¹/₂ pint/1¹/₄ cups oil

2 tsp onion seeds

6 curry leaves

200 g/7 oz/3 cups *parva* (flaked rice)

2 tbsp peanuts

25 g/1 oz/2 tbsp raisins

75 g/2³/₄ oz/5 tbsp sugar

2 tsp salt

2 tsp chilli powder

50 g/2 oz *sev* (optional)

---

1 Rinse and soak the *chana dhaal* in a bowl of water for at least 3 hours.

2 Heat the oil in a saucepan. Add the onion seeds and the curry leaves and fry, stirring constantly, until the onion seeds are crisp and golden.

3 Add the *parva* (flaked rice) to the mixture in the pan and fry until crisp and golden (do not allow to burn).

4 Remove the mixture from the pan and leave

to drain on paper towels so that any excess oil is soaked up.

5 Fry the peanuts in the remaining oil, stirring.

6 Add the peanuts to the flaked rice mixture, stirring to mix well.

7 Add the raisins, sugar, salt and chilli powder and mix together. Mix in the *sev* (if using). Transfer to a serving dish.

8 Re-heat the oil remaining in the pan

and fry the soaked *chana dhaal* until golden. Add to the other ingredients in the serving dish and mix together.

9 This dish can be eaten straight away or stored in an airtight container until you need it.

COOK'S TIP

Sev are very thin sticks made of gram flour which can be bought in Indian and Pakistani grocers.

Deep-Fried Diamond Pastries

Serves 4

INGREDIENTS

150 g/5¹/₂ oz/1 cup plain (all-purpose) flour	¹/₂ tsp salt	300 ml/¹/₂ pint/1¹/₄ cups oil
1 tsp baking powder	1 tbsp black cumin seeds	
	100 ml/3¹/₂ fl oz/¹/₂ cup water	

1 Place the flour in a large mixing bowl.

2 Add the baking powder, salt and the black cumin seeds and stir to mix.

3 Add the water to the dry ingredients and mix to form a soft, elasticated dough.

4 Roll out the dough on to a clean work surface (counter) until about 6 mm/¹/₄ inch thick.

5 Using a sharp knife, score the dough to form diamond shapes.

Re-roll the dough and cut out more diamond shapes until all of the dough has been used up.

6 Heat the oil in a large pan to 180°-190°C/ 350°-375°F or until a small cube of bread browns in 30 seconds.

7 Carefully place the pastry diamonds in the oil, in batches if necessary, and deep-fry until golden brown.

8 Remove the diamond pastries with a perforated spoon and leave to drain on paper towels.

Serve with a *dhaal* for dipping or store and serve when required.

COOK'S TIP

Black cumin seeds are used here for their strong aromatic flavour. White cumin seeds may not be used as a substitute.

Hot Salad

Serves 4

| INGREDIENTS |

1/2 medium-sized cauliflower	1/2 cucumber	salt and pepper
1 green (bell) pepper	4 carrots	
1 red (bell) pepper	2 tbsp butter	

1 Rinse the cauliflower and cut into small florets, using a sharp knife.

2 Cut the (bell) peppers into thin slices.

3 Cut the cucumber into thin slices.

4 Peel the carrots and cut them into thin slices.

5 Melt the butter in a large saucepan, stirring constantly so that it doesn't burn.

6 Add the cauliflower, (bell) peppers, cucumber and carrots and

stir-fry for 5-7 minutes. Season with salt and pepper to taste, cover the pan with a lid, reduce the heat and leave to simmer for about 3 minutes.

7 Transfer the vegetables to a serving dish, toss to mix, and serve immediately.

VARIATION

You can replace the vegetables in this recipe with those of your choice, if you prefer.

COOK'S TIP

In India, you can buy snacks and accompaniments along the roadside while elsewhere you can either buy them from Indian or Pakistani grocers. However, they are fresher and more satisfying made at home.

Cool Cucumber Salad

Serves 4

INGREDIENTS

225 g/8 oz cucumber
1 green chilli (optional)
fresh coriander (cilantro)
   leaves, finely chopped

2 tbsp lemon juice
1/2 tsp salt
1 tsp sugar

fresh mint leaves and red (bell)
   pepper strips, to garnish

1 Using a sharp knife, slice the cucumber thinly. Arrange the cucumber slices on a round serving plate.

2 Using a sharp knife, chop the green chilli (if using).

3 Scatter the chopped chilli over the cucumber.

4 To make the dressing, place the chopped coriander (cilantro) leaves, lemon juice, salt and sugar into a bowl, mix together and set aside.

5 Place the cucumber in the refrigerator and leave to chill for at least 1 hour, or until required.

6 Transfer the cucumber to a serving bowl.

7 Pour the dressing over the cucumber and garnish with mint leaves and (bell) pepper strips.

COOK'S TIP

To store fresh coriander (cilantro), put the roots in a glass of water and keep in a cool place for up to 4 days.

COOK'S TIP

Much of the heat in Indian dishes comes from fresh green chillies, although dried and ground red chillies are also commonplace. In southern India, with its searingly hot temperatures, large quantities of chillies are used because they cause the body to perspire, which has a cooling effect. Numerous varieties of fresh chilli grow in India. As a general rule, the smaller the chilli, the hotter it will be. Fresh chillies will keep for about 5 days in the refrigerator.

Chick-Pea (Garbanzo Bean) Salad

Serves 4

INGREDIENTS

400 g/14 oz can chick-peas (garbanzo beans)	1 medium cucumber	1 red (bell) pepper, sliced
4 carrots	1/2 tsp salt	
1 bunch spring onions (scallions)	1/2 tsp pepper	
	3 tbsp lemon juice	

1 Drain the chick-peas (garbanzo beans) and pour them into a large salad bowl.

2 Using a sharp knife, peel and slice the carrots.

3 Cut the spring onions (scallions) into small, even pieces.

4 Cut the cucumber into thick quarters.

5 Add the sliced carrots, spring onions (scallions) and cucumber

to the chick-peas (garbanzo beans) and mix.

6 Season with the salt and pepper and sprinkle with the lemon juice.

7 Toss the salad ingredients together gently in the bowl using 2 serving spoons.

8 Using a sharp knife, slice the red (bell) pepper thinly.

9 Arrange the slices of red (bell) pepper on

top of the chick-pea (garbanzo bean) salad. Serve the salad immediately or leave to chill in the refrigerator and serve when required.

COOK'S TIP

Using canned chick-peas (garbanzo beans) rather than the dried ones speeds up the cooking time.

Raitas

Serves 4

INGREDIENTS

MINT RAITA:
200 ml/7 fl oz/³/4 cup natural
    yogurt
50 ml/2 fl oz/4 tbsp water
1 small onion, finely chopped
¹/2 tsp mint sauce
¹/2 tsp salt
3 fresh mint leaves, to garnish

CUCUMER RAITA:
225 g/8 oz cucumber
1 medium onion
¹/2 tsp salt
¹/2 tsp mint sauce
300 ml/10 fl oz/1¹/4 cups
    yogurt
150 ml/¹/4 pint/²/3 cup water
fresh mint leaves, to garnish

AUBERGINE (EGGPLANT)
    RAITA:
1 medium aubergine
    (eggplant)
1 tsp salt
1 small onion, finely chopped
2 green chillies, finely chopped
200 ml/7 fl oz/³/4 cup natural
    yogurt
3 tbsp water

1 To make the mint raita,
place the yogurt in a
bowl and whisk with a
fork. Gradually add the
water, whisking well. Add
the onion, mint sauce and
salt and blend together.
Garnish with the fresh
mint leaves.

2 To make the cucumber
raita, peel and slice the
cucumber. Using a sharp
knife, chop the onion

finely. Place the cucumber
and onion in a large bowl,
then add the salt and the
mint sauce. Add the yogurt
and the water and place the
mixture in a liquidizer and
blend well. Transfer to a
serving bowl and serve
garnished with a few fresh
mint leaves.

3 To make the aubergine
(eggplant) raita, rinse
the aubergine (eggplant)

and remove the top end.
Discard the top and chop
the rest into small pieces.
Boil the pieces in a pan of
water until soft. Drain and
mash. Transfer to a serving
bowl and add the salt, the
onion and green chillies,
mixing well. Whip the
yogurt with the water in a
separate bowl and pour
over the aubergine
(eggplant) mixture. Mix
well and serve.

Mango Chutney

Serves 4

INGREDIENTS

1 kg/2 lb 4 oz raw mangoes	2 tsp fresh ginger root, finely	75 g/2³/4 oz/¹/2 cup raisins
4 tbsp salt	chopped	100 g/3¹/2 oz/¹/2 cup dates,
600 ml/1 pint/2¹/2 cups water	2 tsp fresh garlic, crushed	stoned
450 g/1 lb/2¹/3 cups sugar	2 tsp chilli powder	
450 ml/³/4 pint/2 cups vinegar	2 cinnamon sticks	

1 Using a sharp knife, peel, halve and stone the mangoes. Cut the mango flesh into cubes. Place the mango in a large bowl. Add the salt and water and leave overnight. Drain the liquid from the mangoes and set aside.

2 Bring the sugar and vinegar to the boil in a large saucepan over a low heat, stirring.

3 Gradually add the mango cubes, stirring to coat the mango in the sugar and vinegar mixture.

4 Add the ginger, garlic, chilli powder, cinnamon sticks, raisins and the dates, and bring to the boil again, stirring occasionally. Reduce the heat and cook for about 1 hour or until the mixture thickens. Remove from the heat and leave to cool.

5 Remove the cinnamon sticks and discard.

6 Spoon the chutney into clean dry jars and cover tightly with lids. Leave in a cool place for the flavours to fully develop.

COOK'S TIP

When choosing mangoes, select ones that are shiny with unblemished skins. To test if they are ripe, gently cup the mango in your hand and squeeze it gently – it should give slightly to the touch if ready for eating.

Sesame Seed Chutney

Serves 4

INGREDIENTS

8 tbsp sesame seeds	1/2 bunch fresh coriander	1 tsp salt
2 tbsp water	(cilantro)	2 tsp lemon juice
	3 fresh green chillies, chopped	chopped red chilli, to garnish

1 Place the sesame seeds in a large, heavy-based saucepan and dry roast.

2 Set the sesame seeds aside to cool.

3 Once cooled, place the sesame seeds in a food processor or pestle and mortar and grind to form a fine powder.

4 Add the water to the sesame seeds and mix together to form a smooth paste.

5 Using a sharp knife, finely chop the coriander (cilantro).

6 Add the chillies and coriander (cilantro) to the sesame seed paste and grind once again.

7 Add the salt and lemon juice to the mixture and grind again.

8 Remove the mixture from the food processor or pestle and mortar. Transfer to a serving dish and garnish.

COOK'S TIP

Rinsing raw onions with water takes the edge off the raw taste.

COOK'S TIP

Dry roasting coaxes all of the flavour out of dried spices and gives dishes well-harmonized flavours that do not taste raw. Dry roasting only takes a few minutes and you will be able to tell when the spices are ready because of the wonderful fragrance that develops. Be sure to stir the spices constantly and never take your eyes off the pan because the spices can burn very quickly.

Tamarind Chutney

Serves 4-6

INGREDIENTS

2 tbsp tamarind paste
5 tbsp water
1 tsp chilli powder
1/2 tsp ground ginger

1/2 tsp salt
1 tsp sugar
finely chopped coriander
    (cilantro) leaves, to garnish

1 Place the tamarind paste into a mixing bowl.

2 Gradually add the water to the tamarind paste, gently whisking with a fork to form a smooth, runny paste.

3 Add the chilli powder and the ginger to the mixture and blend well.

4 Add the salt and the sugar and mix well.

5 Transfer the chutney to a serving dish and garnish with the coriander (cilantro) leaves.

COOK'S TIP

Chilli powder, or cayenne pepper, is a very fiery spice that should be used with caution.

COOK'S TIP

Vegetable dishes are often given a sharp, sour flavour with the addition of tamarind. This is made from the semi-dried, compressed pulp of the tamarind tree. You can buy bars of the pungent-smelling pulp in Indian and oriental grocery stores. Store it in a tightly sealed plastic bag or airtight container. Alternatively, for greater convenience, keep a jar of tamarind paste in your storecupboard.

Desserts

Indian meals, usually end with something sweet, just as they do in the West. Indian desserts are quite rich and very sweet, so it is a good idea to offer a choice of fresh fruit – mangoes, guavas or melon, for example – as well. These are best served chilled, especially in the summer months.

Among Indian people, desserts such as Indian Bread Pudding, Carrot Dessert and Indian Vermicelli Dessert are served only for special occasions, such as a religious festival. In this chapter, I have also included some simple desserts such as Indian Rice Pudding as well as the more elaborate desserts. Do try some of these dishes, I find that because few restaurants offer much in the way of special Indian desserts they are usually a complete revelation to my Western guests – and always a pleasant one!

Almond Slices

Serves 6-8

INGREDIENTS

3 medium eggs
75 g/2³/4 oz/¹/2 cup ground
almonds
200 g/7 oz/1¹/2 cups milk
powder

200 g/7 oz/1 cup sugar
¹/2 tsp saffron strands
100 g/3¹/2 oz/8 tbsp unsalted
butter

25 g/1 oz/1 tbsp flaked
almonds

1 Beat the eggs together in a bowl and set aside.

2 Place the ground almonds, milk powder, sugar and saffron in a large mixing bowl and stir to mix well.

3 Melt the butter in a small saucepan.

4 Pour the melted butter over the dry ingredients and mix well with a fork.

5 Add the reserved beaten eggs to the almond mixture and stir to blend well.

6 Spread the mixture in a shallow 15-20 cm/ 7-9 inch ovenproof dish and bake in a pre-heated oven at 160°C/325°F/Gas Mark 3 for 45 minutes. Test whether the cake is cooked through by piercing with the tip of a knife or a skewer – it will come out clean if it is cooked thoroughly.

7 Once it had cooled, cut the almond cake into even slices.

8 Decorate the almond slices with flaked almonds and transfer them to serving plates. Serve hot or cold.

COOK'S TIP

These almond slices are best eaten hot but they may also be served cold. They can be made a day or even a week in advance and re-heated. They also freeze beautifully.

Sweet Potato Dessert

Serves 8-10

INGREDIENTS

1 kg/2 lb 4 oz sweet potatoes	175 g/6 oz/1³/₄ cups sugar	a few chopped almonds, to
850 ml/1¹/₂ pints/3¹/₂ cups milk		decorate

1 Using a sharp knife, peel the sweet potatoes. Rinse the sweet potatoes and cut them into slices.

2 Place the sweet potato slices in a large saucepan. Cover with 600 ml/1 pint/2¹/₂ cups milk and cook slowly until the sweet potato is soft enough to be mashed.

3 Remove the sweet potatoes from the heat and mash thoroughly to remove all the lumps.

4 Add the sugar and the remaining 250 ml/¹/₂ pint/1 cup milk to the mashed sweet potatoes, and carefully stir to blend together.

5 Return the pan to the heat and leave the mixture to simmer until it starts to thicken (it should reach the consistency of a cream of chicken soup).

6 Transfer the sweet potato dessert to a serving dish.

7 Decorate the sweet potato dessert with the chopped almonds and serve warm.

COOK'S TIP

Sweet potatoes are longer than ordinary potatoes and have a pinkish or yellowish skin with yellow or white flesh. As their name suggests, they taste slightly sweet.

Deep-Fried Sweetmeats in Syrup

Serves 6-8

INGREDIENTS

5 tbsp dried full-cream milk
    powder
1 1/2 tbsp plain (all-purpose)
    flour
1 tsp baking powder
1 1/2 tbsp unsalted butter
1 medium egg

1 tsp milk to mix (if required)
10 tbsp pure or vegetable ghee

SYRUP:
750 ml/1 1/4 pints/3 1/4 cups
    water
8 tbsp sugar

2 green cardamoms, peeled,
    with seeds crushed
1 large pinch saffron strands
2 tbsp rosewater

1 Place the dried full-cream milk powder, flour and baking powder in a bowl.

2 Place the butter in a pan and heat until melted, stirring.

3 Whisk the egg in a bowl. Add the melted butter and whisked egg to the dry ingredients and blend with a fork (add the teaspoon of extra milk at this stage if necessary) to form a soft dough.

4 Break the dough into about 12 small pieces and shape, in the palms of your hands, into small, smooth balls.

5 Heat the ghee in a deep frying-pan (skillet). Reduce the heat and start frying the dough balls, about 3-4 at a time, tossing and turning gently with a perforated spoon until a dark golden brown colour. Remove the sweetmeats from the pan and set aside in a deep serving bowl.

6 To make the syrup, boil the water and sugar in a pan for 7-10 minutes. Add the crushed cardamom seeds and saffron, and pour over the sweetmeats.

7 Pour the rosewater sparingly over the top. Leave to soak for about 10 minutes in order for the sweetmeats to soak up some of the syrup. Serve hot or cold.

Rice Pudding

Serves 8-10

INGREDIENTS

75 g/2³/4 oz/¹/4 cup basmati rice

1.2 litres/2 pints/5 cups milk
8 tbsp sugar

varq (silver leaf) or chopped pistachio nuts, to decorate

1 Rinse the rice and place in a saucepan. Add 1 pint/ 600 ml/ 2¹/2 cups milk and bring to the boil over a very low heat. Cook until the milk has been completely absorbed by the rice, stirring occasionally.

2 Remove the pan from the heat. Mash the rice, making swift, round movements in the pan, for at least 5 minutes until all of the lumps have been removed.

3 Return the pan to the heat and gradually add the remaining 1 pint/ 600 ml/2¹/2 cups milk. Bring to the boil over a low heat, stirring occasionally.

4 Add the sugar and continue to cook, stirring constantly, for 7-10 minutes or until the mixture is quite thick in consistency.

5 Transfer the rice pudding to a heatproof serving bowl. Decorate with *varq* (silver leaf) or chopped pistachio nuts and serve on its own or with Pooris (see page 236).

COOK'S TIP

Varq is edible silver that is used to decorate elaborate dishes for the most special occasions in India. It is pure silver that has been beaten until it is wafer thin. It comes with a piece of backing paper which is peeled off as the varq is laid on the cooked food. It is extremely delicate and so must be handled with great care. You can buy varq in Indian food stores, and because it is pure silver it should be stored in an airtight bag or box so that it does not tarnish.

Pistachio Dessert

Serves 4–6

INGREDIENTS

850 ml/1$\frac{1}{2}$ pints/3$\frac{1}{2}$ cups
   water
250 g/9 oz/3 cups pistachio
   nuts
250 g/9 oz/1$\frac{3}{4}$ cups full-
   cream dried milk powder

450 g/1 lb/2$\frac{1}{3}$ cups sugar
2 cardamoms, with seeds
   crushed
2 tbsp rosewater
a few strands saffron

fresh mint leaves, to decorate

1 Boil about 1 pint/
600 ml water in a
saucepan. Remove the pan
from the heat and soak the
pistachios in this water for
about 5 minutes. Drain and
remove the skins.

2 Grind the pistachios in
a food processor or
pestle and mortar.

3 Add the dried milk
powder to the ground
pistachios and mix well.

4 To make the syrup,
place the remaining

300 ml/$\frac{1}{2}$ pint water and
the sugar in a pan and heat
gently. When the liquid
begins to thicken, add the
cardamom seeds, rosewater
and saffron.

5 Add the syrup to the
pistachio mixture and
cook for about 5 minutes,
stirring, until the mixture
thickens. Set the mixture
aside and leave to cool
slightly.

6 Once cooled enough to
handle, roll the
mixture into balls (use up

all of the pistachio
mixture). Decorate with
a few fresh mint leaves
and leave to set before
serving.

COOK'S TIP

*It is best to buy whole
pistachio nuts and grind
them yourself, rather than
using packets of ready-
ground nuts. Freshly ground
nuts have the best flavour as
grinding releases their
natural oils.*

Pooris stuffed with Chana Dhaal Halva

Makes 10

INGREDIENTS

POORIS:
200 g/7 oz/1 cup coarse
    semolina
100 g/3$^{1}/_{2}$ oz/$^{3}/_{4}$ cup plain
    (all-purpose) flour
$^{1}/_{2}$ tsp salt
1$^{1}/_{2}$ tbsp ghee, plus extra for
    frying

150 ml/$^{1}/_{4}$ pint/$^{2}/_{3}$ cup milk

FILLING:
8 tbsp *chana dhaal*
850 ml/1$^{1}/_{2}$ pints/3$^{1}/_{2}$ cups
    water
5 tbsp ghee
2 green cardamoms, peeled

4 cloves
8 tbsp sugar
2 tbsp ground almonds
$^{1}/_{2}$ tsp saffron strands
50 g/1$^{3}/_{4}$ oz/$^{1}/_{4}$ cup sultanas

1 To make the *pooris*, place the semolina, flour and salt in a bowl and mix. Add the ghee and rub in with your fingers. Add the milk and mix to form a dough. Knead the dough for 5 minutes, cover and leave to rise for 3 hours. Then knead on a floured surface for 15 minutes.

2 Roll out the dough and divide into ten portions. Roll these into 12.5 cm/5 inch circles.

3 To make the filling, soak the *chana dhaal* for at least 3 hours. Place in a pan with the water and boil over a medium heat until all the water has evaporated and the *dhaal* is soft enough to be mashed into a paste.

4 In a separate pan, heat the ghee and add the cardamom seeds and cloves. Reduce the heat, add the *chana dhaal* paste and stir, scraping the bottom of the pan, for 5-7 minutes.

5 Fold in the sugar and almonds and stir for 10 minutes. Add the saffron and sultanas and stir until thickened.

6 Spoon the filling on to one half of each pastry round. Dampen the edges with water and fold the other half over to seal.

7 Fry the *pooris* in heated ghee over a low heat until golden. Drain on paper towels and serve.

Indian Bread Pudding

Serves 4-6

INGREDIENTS
---

6 medium slices bread
5 tbsp ghee (preferably pure)
10 tbsp sugar
300 ml/¹/₂ pint/1¹/₄ cups
   water
3 green cardamoms, without
   husks

600 ml/1 pint/2¹/₂ cups milk
175 ml/6 fl oz/³/₄ cup
   evaporated milk or *khoya*
   (see Cook's Tip)
¹/₂ tsp saffron strands

TO DECORATE:
chopped almonds
2 leaves *varq* (silver leaf)
   (optional)

---

1 Cut the bread slices into quarters.

2 Heat the ghee in a frying-pan (skillet) and fry the bread, turning once, until crisp and golden.

3 Place the fried bread in the bottom of a heatproof dish and reserve.

4 To make the syrup, place the sugar, water and cardamom seeds in a pan and bring to the boil until the syrup thickens.

5 Pour the syrup over the fried bread.

6 In a separate pan, bring the milk, evaporated milk or *khoya* (see Cook's Tip) and the saffron to the boil over a low heat until the milk has halved in volume.

7 Pour the milk over the syrup-coated bread.

8 Decorate with chopped almonds and *varq* (if using). Serve the bread

pudding with or without cream.

COOK'S TIP

To make khoya, *boil 900 ml/1¹/₂ pints of milk in a large saucepan, making sure that it doesn't burn. Reduce the heat and boil for 35-40 minutes, stirring occasionally. The milk should reduce to a quarter of its volume, and when completely cooked should resemble a sticky dough.*

Almond Sherbert

Serves 2

INGREDIENTS

225 g/8 oz/2 cups whole almonds	2 tbsp sugar 300 ml/$^1/_2$ pint/1$^1/_4$ cups milk	300 ml/$^1/_2$ pint/1$^1/_4$ cups water

1 Soak the almonds in a bowl of water for at least 3 hours or preferably overnight.

2 Using a sharp knife, chop the almonds into small pieces. Grind to a fine paste in a food processor or with a pestle and mortar.

3 Add the sugar to the almond paste and grind once again to form a fine paste.

4 Add the milk and water and mix together well (in a liquidizer if you have one).

5 Transfer the almond sherbert to a large serving dish.

6 Leave the almond sherbert to chill in the refrigerator for about 30 minutes. Stir the almond sherbert just before serving.

COOK'S TIP

In India, ice-cool sherberts such as this one are served on special occasions, such as religious festivals. They would be served on the very finest tableware and decorated with varq, *the edible silver or gold leaf.*

COOK'S TIP

An electric coffee grinder or spice mill will greatly cut down the time taken to grind the almonds. If using a coffee grinder that is also used for coffee, always remember to clean the grinder thoroughly afterwards, otherwise you will end up with strange-tasting coffee! A pestle and mortar will take longer and is not as good for large quantities.

Coconut Sweet

Serves 4–6

INGREDIENTS

75 g/2³/4 oz/6 tbsp butter
200 g/7 oz/3 cups desiccated
(shredded) coconut

175 ml/6 fl oz/³/4 cup
condensed milk

a few drops of pink food
colouring (optional)

1 Place the butter in a heavy-based saucepan and melt over a low heat, stirring so that the butter doesn't burn on the bottom of the pan.

2 Add the desiccated (shredded) coconut to the melted butter, stirring.

3 Stir in the condensed milk and the pink food colouring (if using) and mix continuously for 7-10 minutes.

4 Remove the saucepan from the heat, set aside and leave the coconut mixture to cool slightly.

5 Once cool enough to handle, shape the coconut mixture into long blocks and cut into equal-sized rectangles. Leave the sweet to set for about 1 hour, then serve.

VARIATION

If you prefer, you could divide the coconut mixture in step 2, and add the drops of pink food colouring to only one half of the mixture. This way, you will have an attractive combination of pink and white coconut sweets.

COOK'S TIP

Coconut is used extensively in Indian cooking to add flavour and creaminess to various dishes. The best flavour comes from freshly grated coconut, although ready-prepared desiccated (shredded) coconut, as used here, makes an excellent stand-by. Freshly grated coconut freezes successfully, so it is well worth preparing when you have the time.

Semolina Dessert

Serves 4

INGREDIENTS

6 tbsp pure ghee
3 whole cloves
3 whole cardamoms
8 tbsp coarse semolina
1/2 tsp saffron

50 g/1³/4 oz/1/2 cup sultanas
10 tbsp sugar
300 ml/1/2 pint/1¹/4 cups
    water
300 ml/1/2 pint/1¹/4 cups milk
cream, to serve

TO DECORATE:
25 g/1 oz/1/2 cup desiccated
    (shredded) coconut,
    toasted
25 g/1 oz/1/4 cup chopped
    almonds
25 g/1 oz/1/4 cup pistachio
    nuts, soaked and chopped
    (optional)

1 Place the ghee in a saucepan and melt over a medium heat.

2 Add the cloves and the whole cardamoms to the melted butter and reduce the heat, stirring to mix.

3 Add the semolina to the spice mixture in the saucepan and stir-fry until the semolina turns a little darker.

4 Add the saffron, sultanas and the sugar to the semolina mixture, stirring to mix well.

5 Pour in the water and milk and stir-fry the mixture continuously until the semolina has softened. Add a little more water if required.

6 Remove the pan from the heat. Transfer the semolina to a serving dish.

7 Decorate the semolina dessert with the toasted desiccated (shredded) coconut, flaked almonds and pistachios. Serve with a little cream drizzled over the top.

COOK'S TIP

Cloves give flavour and aroma to both sweet and savoury dishes, but should be used sparingly.

Carrot Dessert

Serves 4-6

INGREDIENTS

1.5 kg/3 lb 5 oz carrots
10 tbsp ghee
600 ml/1 pint/2¹/₂ pints milk
175 ml/6 fl oz/³/₄ cup
    evaporated milk or *khoya*
    (see page 238)

10 whole cardamoms, peeled
    and crushed
8-10 tbsp sugar

TO DECORATE:
25 g/1 oz/¹/₄ cup pistachio
    nuts, chopped
2 leaves *varq* (silver leaf)
    (optional)

1 Rinse, peel and grate the carrots.

2 Heat the ghee in a large, heavy saucepan.

3 Add the grated carrots to the ghee and stir-fry for 15-20 minutes or until the moisture from the carrots has evaporated and the carrots have darkened in colour.

4 Add the milk, evaporated milk or *khoya*, cardamoms and sugar to the carrot mixture

and continue to stir-fry for a further 30-35 minutes, until it is a rich brownish-red colour.

5 Transfer the mixture to a large shallow dish.

6 Decorate with the pistachio nuts and *varq* (if using) and serve at once.

COOK'S TIP

A quicker way to grate the carrots is to use a food processor.

COOK'S TIP

I like to use pure ghee for this dessert as it is rather special and tastes better made with pure ghee. However, if you are trying to limit your fat intake, use vegetable ghee instead.

Sweet Saffron Rice

Serves 4

INGREDIENTS

200 g/7 oz/1 cup basmati rice	2 tbsp ghee	TO DECORATE:
200 g/7 oz/1 cup sugar	3 cloves	a few pistachio nuts (optional)
1 pinch saffron strands	3 cardamoms	*varq* (silver leaf) (optional)
300 ml/¹/₂ pint/1¹/₄ cups water	25 g/1 oz/2 tbsp sultanas	

1 Rinse the rice twice and bring to the boil in a saucepan of water, stirring. Remove the pan from the heat when the rice is half-cooked, drain the rice and set aside.

2 In a separate saucepan, boil the sugar and saffron in the water, stirring, until the syrup thickens. Set aside.

3 In another saucepan, heat the ghee, cloves and cardamoms, stirring occasionally. Remove the pan from the heat.

4 Return the rice to a low heat and add the sultanas, stirring well to combine.

5 Pour the syrup over the rice mixture and stir.

6 Pour the ghee mixture over the rice and leave to simmer over a low heat for 10-15 minutes. Check to see whether the rice is cooked; if not, add a little water, cover and leave to simmer gently.

7 Serve warm, decorated with pistachio nuts and

varq (silver leaf), and with cream if desired.

VARIATION

For a slightly stronger saffron flavour, place the saffron strands on a small piece of kitchen foil and toast them lightly under a hot grill (broiler) for a few moments (take care not to overcook them or the flavour will spoil) and crush finely between your fingers before adding to the sugar and water in step 2.

Ground Almonds Cooked in Ghee & Milk

Serves 2-4

INGREDIENTS

2 tbsp vegetable or pure ghee
25 g/1 oz/¼ cup plain (all-purpose) flour

100 g/3½ oz/½ cup ground almonds
300 ml/½ pint/1¼ cups milk
50 g/1¾ oz/¼ cup sugar

fresh mint leaves, to decorate

1 Place the ghee in a small, heavy-based saucepan. Melt the ghee over a gentle heat, stirring so that it doesn't burn.

2 Reduce the heat and add the flour, stirring the mixture vigorously to remove any lumps.

3 Add the almonds to the ghee and flour mixture, stirring continuously.

4 Gradually add the milk and sugar to the mixture in the pan and bring to the boil. Continue cooking for 3-5 minutes or until the liquid is smooth and reaches the consistency of cream of chicken soup.

5 Transfer to a serving dish, decorate and serve hot.

VARIATION

You could use coconut milk in this recipe, for a delicious alternative.

COOK'S TIP

Ghee comes in two forms and can be bought from Asian grocers. It is worth noting that pure ghee, made from melted butter, is not suitable for vegans, although there is a vegetable ghee available from Indian grocers and some health-food stores.

Indian Vermicelli Pudding

Serves 4-6

INGREDIENTS

25 g/1 oz pistachio nuts
  (optional)
25 g/1 oz flaked almonds
3 tbsp ghee
100 g/3½ oz/1½ cups
  seviyan (Indian vermicelli)

850 ml/1½ pints/3½ cups
  milk
175 ml/6 fl oz/¾ cup
  evaporated milk

8 tbsp sugar
6 dates, stoned and dried

1 Soak the pistachio nuts (if using) in a bowl of water for at least 3 hours. Peel the pistachios and mix them with the flaked almonds. Chop the nuts finely and set aside.

2 Melt the ghee in a large saucepan and lightly fry the *seviyan* (Indian vermicelli). Reduce the heat immediately (the *seviyan* will turn golden brown very quickly so be careful not to burn it), and if necessary remove the pan from the heat (do not worry if some bits are a little darker than others).

3 Add the milk to the *seviyan* (Indian vermicelli) and bring to the boil slowly, taking care that it does not boil over.

4 Add the evaporated milk, sugar and the stoned dates to the mixture in the pan. Leave to simmer for 10 minutes, uncovered, stirring occasionally. When the consistency starts to thicken, pour the pudding into a serving bowl.

5 Decorate the pudding with the chopped pistachio nuts and flaked almonds.

COOK'S TIP

You will find seviyan *(Indian vermicelli) in Indian grocers. This dessert can be served warm or cold.*

Almond & Pistachio Dessert

Serves 4–6

INGREDIENTS

75 g/2³/4 oz/6 tbsp unsalted butter
200 g/7 oz/1 cup ground almonds

150 ml/5 fl oz/²/3 cup single (light) cream
200 g/7 oz/1 cup sugar
8 almonds, chopped

10 pistachio nuts, chopped

1 Place the butter in a medium-sized saucepan, preferably non-stick. Melt the butter, stirring well.

2 Gradually add the ground almonds, cream and sugar to the melted butter in the pan, stirring to combine. Reduce the heat and stir the mixture constantly for 10-12 minutes, scraping the bottom of the pan.

3 Increase the heat until the mixture turns a little darker in colour.

4 Transfer the almond mixture to a shallow serving dish and smooth the top with the back of a spoon.

5 Decorate the top of the dessert with the chopped almonds and pistachios.

6 Leave the dessert to set for about 1 hour, then cut into diamond shapes and serve cold.

COOK'S TIP

This almond dessert can be made in advance and stored in an airtight container in the refrigerator for several days.

COOK'S TIP

You could use a variety of shaped pastry cutters, to cut the dessert into different shapes, rather than diamonds, if you prefer.

Index